"If there is anything that I truly believe in other than God and family, it's the importance of female friendship in a woman's life. It really is the thing that has helped me maintain my sanity over the course of my life. But it can be a tricky road to navigate, especially as we get older and our lives become more busy than they were before. That's why I love what Amy and Jess have written in these pages. They are real and honest about what friendship means, how hard it can be, and yet they give practical, real advice on how to connect with the people around us. They are funny and engaging and this book will make you feel like you're sitting at a table with friends you trust, breaking it all down. I promise you'll turn the last page and be better for having read their words."

—MELANIE SHANKLE, NEW YORK TIMES BESTSELLING
AUTHOR OF NOBODY'S CUTER THAN YOU

"It never fails, when I read the writings of Amy and Jess, I pull out my journal and highlighter. There are treasure troves of wisdom and affirmations peppered throughout each page. I cackled out loud, I nodded my head, and more than once I yelled, 'Yes, THAT!' Maybe that's the most beautiful gift that Amy and Jess possess: their love for humanity rises off the page—when you read, you feel like their friend. Amy and Jess teach about friendships in the most honest and humble way possible: by becoming the friend each of their readers truly longs to have."

—MARY KATHERINE BACKSTROM, NATIONAL BESTSELLING AUTHOR OF
HOLY HOT MESS: FINDING GOD IN THE DETAILS OF THIS WEIRD AND WONDERFUL LIFE

"With an epidemic of loneliness sweeping through our hearts and homes, this book offers an energizing glimpse at what true connection can look like. Funny, refreshingly honest, and super practical, it's the fresh take on friendship that we've all been looking for."

—MANDY ARIOTO, PRESIDENT AND CEO OF MOPS INTERNATIONAL

"Everything Amy and Jess write is powerful (and viral, in a good way), so I wasn't surprised to love their book, *I'll Be There (But I'll Be Wearing Sweatpants)*. These pages are filled with compassion, truth, and their signature humor. I loved it. Thank you, Amy and Jess, for reminding me that authentic friendship is attainable for us all."

—LESLIE MEANS, FOUNDER AND OWNER HER VIEW FROM HOME

I'll Be There

(But I'll Be Wearing Sweatpants)

I'll Be There

(BUT I'LL BE WEARING SWEATPANTS)

FINDING UNFILTERED, REAL-LIFE FRIENDSHIPS IN THIS CRAZY, CHAOTIC WORLD

AMY WEATHERLY AND JESS JOHNSTON

NELSON BOOKS

An Imprint of Thomas Nelson

I'll Be There (But I'll Be Wearing Sweatpants)

© 2022 by Amy Weatherly and Jess Johnston

All rights reserved. No portion of this book may be reproduced, stored in a retrieval system, or transmitted in any form or by any means—electronic, mechanical, photocopy, recording, scanning, or other—except for brief quotations in critical reviews or articles, without the prior written permission of the publisher.

Published in Nashville, Tennessee, by Nelson Books, an imprint of Thomas Nelson. Nelson Books and Thomas Nelson are registered trademarks of HarperCollins Christian Publishing, Inc.

Thomas Nelson titles may be purchased in bulk for educational, business, fundraising, or sales promotional use. For information, please email SpecialMarkets@ThomasNelson.com.

Unless otherwise noted, Scripture quotations are taken from the Holy Bible, New International Version®, NIV®. Copyright © 1973, 1978, 1984, 2011 by Biblica, Inc.® Used by permission of Zondervan. All rights reserved worldwide. www.zondervan.com. The "NIV" and "New International Version" are trademarks registered in the United States Patent and Trademark Office by Biblica, Inc.®

Scripture quotations marked NLT are taken from the Holy Bible, New Living Translation. Copyright © 1996, 2004, 2015 by Tyndale House Foundation. Used by permission of Tyndale House Ministries, Carol Stream, Illinois 60188. All rights reserved.

Any internet addresses, phone numbers, or company or product information printed in this book are offered as a resource and are not intended in any way to be or to imply an endorsement by Thomas Nelson, nor does Thomas Nelson vouch for the existence, content, or services of these sites, phone numbers, companies, or products beyond the life of this book.

Library of Congress Cataloging-in-Publication Data

Names: Weatherly, Amy, 1983- author. | Johnston, Jess, 1985- author.
Title: I'll be there (but I'll be wearing sweatpants): finding unfiltered, real-life friendships in this crazy, chaotic world / Amy Weatherly and Jess Johnston.
Description: Nashville, Tennessee : Nelson Books, [2022] | Summary: "Amy Weatherly and Jess Johnston, founders of the wildly popular "Sister, I Am with You" online community, address common obstacles to true connection and offer a confessional, hilarious, and practical guide for building deep friendships in the middle of this crazy, rollercoaster life"-- Provided by publisher.
Identifiers: LCCN 2021034590 (print) | LCCN 2021034591 (ebook) | ISBN 9781400226757 (trade paperback) | ISBN 9781400226795 (ebook)
Subjects: LCSH: Female friendship.
Classification: LCC HM1161 .W43 2022 (print) | LCC HM1161 (ebook) | DDC 302.34082--dc23
LC record available at https://lccn.loc.gov/2021034590
LC ebook record available at https://lccn.loc.gov/2021034591

Printed in the United States of America

22 23 24 25 26   LSC   10 9 8 7 6 5 4 3

Amy: To C, B, and M, who have changed me and inspired me since the day you were born. This book is for you three. Love Jesus. Know yourself. Do life with people. And remember that wherever the road takes you, whichever path you choose, I'm here for it. I'm here for you and I'm cheering you on wildly from the sidelines. I love you through the moon. (But please learn to throw away your trash, okay? I'm really tired of picking it up.)

To Brandon, who has kept me laughing from day one. Thank you for basically locking me out of the house and forcing me to go write even when I wanted to sit on the couch and pretend like deadlines didn't exist. None of this would have happened if you hadn't lovingly nagged me. You are my home and my favorite person on this planet.

To my mom and dad. Your support has meant everything.

To the friends who have showed up, stayed with me, and taken me exactly as I am. I could never thank you enough. You make life so full and so fun and I am so, so grateful. You know who you are.

.««-

Jess: To Graham, who championed me and believed in me before I believed in myself. To my mom, who inspired me to be a writer, and my dad, who thinks I'm amazing even when I'm not. To my friends new and old, who have been the inspiration behind every word of this book. To Malachi, Scout, Oaklee, and Haven—I pray you build amazing friendships throughout your lives (and sorry about all the screen time and frozen pizza while I wrote this book).

To every girl and woman who has ever felt alone, may this book be the beginning of a beautiful journey to friendship.

CONTENTS

INTRODUCTION

We didn't write this book alone. We could have. Both of us are fully capable of penning these lessons and scripting these stories all on our own, but we didn't want to. In our guts, we knew it wasn't supposed to be a solo effort. It was supposed to be done together.

We knew there was something beautiful and significant and poignant about birthing this book on friendship through the work of our own friendship.

We love how this friendship has grown us and how it has carried us through some tough times. We love how this friendship has endured, and we love how it came to be.

It wasn't by accident.

We connected through blogging groups, and it didn't take us long to realize we were cut from the same cloth. We quickly bonded over our love of the Enneagram, Mexican food, going commando in leggings, and sharing way too much information with people we hardly know.

Our first conversations were hours long. We talked about everything from pop culture to whether Topo Chico or La Croix was better. We found it natural to chat and to laugh, and we found it equally easy to dig into the nitty-gritty of our lives and hearts.

We built safety and trust as we shared our real-life struggles and our real-life desires, particularly on the topic of sisterhood.

As the days and months passed and our friendship grew, we talked about how independent the world had become and how much we longed to make a difference.

We talked about our heartbreaks, our years spent in loneliness, and all the times we wondered what the heck was so wrong with us that we didn't have any friends. We talked about our stories of redemption and how we had both come to build some amazing friendships.

We dreamed of conferences and speaking on stages. We dreamed of books and communities and giving women a space to come alive, a space to feel accepted, and a space to feel secure. And we dreamed of strong relationships—the kind of relationships we knew these women craved deep down.

And before we knew it, our own tiny corner of the internet—Sister, I Am With You—came to be.

We poured into that place. We prayed over that place. We wrote our hearts out. We watched this tiny spark become a fire, and we watched that fire grow and burn and light up women from all over the world, from all different ages and walks of life.

Every word of this book was born from our hearts, our stories of struggle and loneliness as well as precious friendships. But this book was also born from *our* friendship. It was born through late-night texts of "I don't think I can do this." It was born through a hundred phone calls of laughing, venting, and encouraging. It was born through "It's going to be okay, I promise" and "We can do this, I'm sure." It was born through "Have I told you lately how much I love you and how amazing you are?" It was born through random selfies of our double chins just to make each other laugh. It was born through flowers sent just because. It was born through a surprise package of Ted Lasso stickers, and it was born in the year 2020 when absolutely everything was in upheaval and we needed sisterhood more than ever.

The message of this book is simple: let's not do life alone; let's do it together. And that's exactly how this book was written—together.

We can honestly tell you that although we *could have* written it separately, this book is a million times more beautiful because we created it with each other.

We don't know what your story has been; we don't know what brought you here today; we don't know what heartbreaks you've suffered; we don't know what beautiful friendships you've had and have. All we know is we're so glad you're here.

This is our prayer for you:

Dear Jesus,

We pray for the one who is lonely. We've been there, and we've felt it. We know how excruciating it can be.

We pray for the one who wonders if she's too much, not enough, and for all the women who teeter-totter back and forth between these two extremes.

Show her that there's nothing wrong with her; she just hasn't met the right people yet.

Show her that she is held, that she's victorious, and that she's your most marvelous creation. Encourage her heart, and fill up her mind with all the beautiful thoughts you have for her. Let her know we need her here because what she brings is priceless and unique.

We pray for the one who feels defeated, for the one who doesn't know how to begin, and for the one who is exhausted. Would you bring her peace? Would you bring her comfort? Would you bring her friends? Highlight the ones she should pursue, and let there be opportunities to meet new people in the most unexpected ways. Give her the bravery it takes to be authentic, and vulnerable, and real, and give her the courage to try.

We pray for the one who has a broken heart and wounded wings and is afraid to fly again. Patch her up. Wrap her in care, and set her free.

And most of all, help her feel completely loved—from the top of her messy bun to the bottom of her feet, even her toenails that badly need a pedicure.

Shower her with grace and an abundance of rest. Fill her heart with hope and her mind with peace, and let her wake up with energy, excitement, and the very fullest of hearts.

Let this book meet her where she is. Use the stories to help her feel seen and these words to help her feel valued. Let the things she finds here stick with her, and let them change her.

And please, let this book help her smile too.

Amen.

love,
Amy and Jess

1

When You Really Need a Friend (Yeah, Us Too)

love, Jess and Amy

Oh hey, we're Jess and Amy. We want to talk about friend-ship, but we're not just talking about the kind of friendship that puts on lipstick and pants with zippers and orders something fancy at a nice restaurant (although that's fun sometimes). We're talking about the kind of friendship that gets raw and gritty. The kind of friendship that is built for real life and running errands. The kind of friendship that is safe for big feelings, deep secrets, and laughing so hard you snort. The kind of friendship that stays through for sickness, health, anxiety, and announcements like "Hey, something is hanging out of your nose."

We're not talking about the kind of friendship that means being with the "in" crowd or being on the VIP list for a party. We're talking about being on the VIP list for the hospital when your friend is having a surgery. We're talking about being on the VIP list for kid birthday parties and movie nights in your sweatpants. We're talking about being the VIP in someone's real, authentic, and true life. We're talking about the kind of friendship that holds up under pressure, the kind that withstands a whole lotta heat. We're talking about the kind of friendship that has an open-door policy when laundry is covering the couch, the sink is full of dishes, and your hair hasn't been washed in a week. Thank goodness for dry shampoo.

We're talking about belonging to each other—like really, really belonging. We're talking about a friendship that isn't just good for the freeway but can pop into four-wheel drive and go off-roading too. A friendship that doesn't have to strive or perform but is comfortable to curl up next to and share your whole truth with—no filters needed.

We're talking about the kind of friendship that makes you actually want to pick up the phone.

We don't know about you, but that's the kind of friendship we've wanted our entire lives, with our whole hearts. We wanted it. We dreamed of it, and yet it felt so far away, so unattainable, especially now as adults.

We felt like we had shown up to the ball in our nastiest pair of sweatpants. (You know, the ones with the hole in the crotchal region. They're not the prettiest, but they're real, worn in, and oh so comfortable. Plus if it's hot, no biggie because you've got that sweet breeze coming in.)

If you've ever walked into a party and instantly felt like the outsider; if you've ever wanted to disappear, sneak away, moonwalk out of the room, or casually park yourself next to the host's pet with a plate of cheese and crackers for the rest of the night—we get it. Us too.

If you've ever become best friends with your barista or your Instacart delivery person because you literally didn't have any other adults to talk to—yep, Jess is raising her hand here. Sister, I am with you. Their names were Anna and Leslie, and they were fantastic listeners. To all the people who were waiting for me to move out of the drive-through line, *excuse me*. Anna needed to know that I'd been having a very hard time lately. Anna got it. Anna cared. Anna also made a mean caramel latte. We were having a moment, and your honking wasn't going to stop us.

If you've ever walked away from meeting someone new and collapsed onto the steering wheel the second you got back into your car because you were pretty sure you'd ruined things with your big fat mouth—yup, Amy's turn to raise her hand. I did this just last week. And I was annoyed at myself the whole way home. *Why did you say that weird thing about finding half-eaten CHEETOS in your bra? This is not normal chitchat. This is borderline disgusting. She is never going to want to hang out with you again.*

If you've ever felt like you weren't enough, like you were too introverted, too boring, too awkward, too average to make any kind of lasting impression, yes, uh-huh, been there. And then we spent the next day thinking of all the witty things we "should" have said. We're very good at conversation after three to five hours of careful planning.

Also, PS: nineties movies really led us to believe we were going to have a Rachel Leigh Cook moment in *She's All That*, only no one ever showed up to take off our glasses and transform us into someone cool. Never mind the fact that we don't wear glasses; we could have bought fakes, you know?

If you've ever felt so bulldozed and blindsided by a friend breakup that you struggled to put your heart out there again, *ouch*, we've been in that same position a time or two. Losing a friend is deeply painful, gut-wrenching even, and it causes you to question yourself, stop trusting others, and put up walls so high and so thick they are almost impossible for anyone to climb over.

We hope it gives you courage to know you're in good company with your feelings. When we think of certain friendships that we lost, our hearts ache like the breakup was just yesterday.

If you've ever felt like you were too much, too extroverted, too prone to overshare, and too likely to overwhelm everyone like a golden retriever that didn't get her fetch time today, us too. Does everyone talk with a girl they literally just met at the park about how many stitches they got giving birth to their firstborn? Yes? No? Okay. Us either. Is it odd for said hypothetical girl to know this information before she even knows your name?

If you've ever put your foot so far down your mouth that you thought your best plan of action would be to move to a new town or, better yet, a new country—yes, yes, and yes. *New Zealand sounds nice. Let's pull up Zillow and see what kind of houses are available. Whew . . . kinda pricey. Scratch that. Canada, anyone?*

If you've ever felt so busy, so overworked, so chaotic that you couldn't imagine how you could possibly make time for friendships, um, yes. Speaking of which, can someone come over and take our kids to the dentist? They have appointments scheduled, but honestly, we don't know exactly when. Whoops.

If you've ever had someone introduce herself to you even though you've met her ten times before, we are your people.

"Hi. I'm _____. I don't think we've ever met."

We have actually met, multiple times, and we go through this exact cat-and-mouse dance every single time. It is so nice to have made such an impression on you. Doesn't hurt at all.

We know the sting of being forgettable, invisible, and completely unseen. Sometimes adult friendship feels exactly like being picked last for dodgeball, and it makes us want to go home and cry too. Your tears are not lost here.

If you have absolutely no idea how to even begin, if you have no idea where to look, and if you can't seem to make the plunge and dive into a friendship with your feelings, yep, we get it. It is scary. You desperately want to invite people in, but what if they turn up their noses and run for the hills the second they see the real you? We've been there, and it's terrifying. Your heart is your most sacred possession. We want to guard ours too.

If you've ever been scrolling through social media only to have your eyes go wide and your stomach jump straight into your throat when you see a picture of everyone together at an outing you weren't invited to—again, yup, we know that feeling. We feel sick just thinking about it.

If you've ever wanted to scream, "But hooooow?!" when someone tells you to "find your people," or if you've ever panicked while filling out a form and realized you don't have an emergency contact, then girl, you're speaking our language. Been there.

If you've ever felt so insecure and so unsure about putting yourself out there that staying home with a bag of barbecue-flavored LAY'S and pajama pants seemed infinitely safer than risking being rejected, same.

This book is a personal invitation into our journeys, our joys, and our discoveries in friendship.

It's our confessional. It's our tell-all. It's our let's-do-this-together. It's our love letter to our daughters, and it's our love letter to our younger selves. We needed this book back then (even more than we needed to lay off the white eyeliner, CK One perfume, and plucking our eyebrows into smithereens), but the truth is, we still need it.

Nobody gave us a handbook on how to deal with friendships when we became adults, so we decided to write our own.

More than anything else, though, this book is our love letter to you.

⋘

We (Amy and Jess) met three years ago. Our messages to each other started with things like "Girl, those earrings on you though" and "Have you ever had a Chick-fil-A sandwich with cheese on it? Because it's life changing FYI." After a month or so we started chatting on the phone. Jess was usually on a run, breathing like she was about to pass out in a ditch (and telling Amy to maybe call 911 if she went silent), and Amy was usually putting on her makeup and telling her kids to please not pee in the cups anymore. Our friendship moved easily from the goofy, the mundane, and the surfacy to the deep, the raw, and the authentic.

Sometimes we'd sit in our cars, Amy in Texas, Jess in California, with our orders of coffee and iced tea after dropping the kids at school. Amy would sing a little Taylor Swift for Jess to hear, and then we'd just talk. We'd put our feet up on the dash and pick at our chipped polish. We'd talk about everything in our lives, but we'd often come back to the topic of friendship.

We agreed that friendship was, and always has been, among our deepest desires.

Friendship has been the cause of some of our lowest lows, but it's also been the cause of some of our highest highs.

We talked about how we'd struggled with it through the years. How we'd both moved and been the "new girl." How we'd found genuine friendship and how much it meant to us. How we'd been hurt and left out. How we'd felt like we were the only ones not given the map to sisterhood.

How we didn't know why it was all so hard.

One day Amy called and said, "Jess, it happened again. I was the only one uninvited to the party, and I'm just sick. I'm sitting alone in my closet crying like I'm thirteen. Why does this still happen? Why does it hurt so much? What is wrong with me? Why don't people like me? It hurts now, but it also hurts because I've been hurt in this exact same way before. Why do I keep getting bumped from the A-list to the B-list to the nonexistent list? It brings me right back to grade school. I hate it so much."

Another day Jess called and said, "Amy, I don't belong. I feel like an outsider when I walk into that room. I just feel like they don't like who I am. It makes me feel so small and unimportant. It takes me right back to that season of postpartum depression."

Yet another day Amy called, sniffling and choking back tears. "Jess, my best friend's moving away. I'm absolutely heartbroken. I'm so happy for her, but I don't know what I'm going to do without her. She is my person. This town isn't going to feel like home without her here. I don't know how to start all over."

We'd sit in our cars or on our couches surrounded by unfolded laundry, telling our kids to please not color on their faces anymore and yelling things like "Who has the Sharpie?! Give it. Give it to me now!" while talking through the deepest, messiest parts of friendship and wondering why we weren't all talking about it more often.

You should know that we didn't write this book because we've always had deep friendships. We didn't write this book because we've always been included and popular (not even a little).

We wrote this book because we've been there, we've felt that, we've written about it in our journals too.

We wrote this book because we've been overlooked and forgotten. We wrote this book because we've each felt the deep and aching pain of loneliness. We wrote this book because we've walked through seasons of being completely and entirely alone. We wrote this book because we've stood in front of the mirror wondering, *What is wrong with me?* We wrote this book because we've felt stuck in our pain with no tools to move forward. We wrote this book because our tears and our sweat are on the field of friendship.

When you were young, you just hung out with people. No big deal. No show. No fancy plates or big, planned-out to-dos. You just hung out and basically did nothing except maybe make some freakishly red Kool-Aid you found deep in your mom's cupboards. It didn't matter what you did because you were together.

We need to simplify things again.

This book isn't a how-to guide to complicated friendship. It's not a ten-step formula to planning some fancy girls' night. It's not about thinking up a theme or worrying about the right outfit (God knows we don't have time for that). Let's shake off those preconceived ideas and imposed expectations. This isn't about impressing anyone. We don't need all that. We think we do, but we don't. Life is hard enough. We just need one another.

The generations before us made time for one another. They hung out with their friends and neighbors and went to church groups on the regular. They got it. They got that connection really matters. They got that the only way to build a solid relationship is to spend time together. It isn't about cooking anything showy or cleaning your ceiling fans. Throw some food on a paper towel and call it a day. Pour some coffee directly into your friends' mouths if all your mugs are dirty. It honestly doesn't matter.

Let's spend time together.

Let's make friendship a priority.

Let's show up and let's genuinely care for one another.

Let's do life for one another and next to one another and with one another.

We've done the fake. We've done the phony. We've forced ourselves to fit in at parties where we didn't belong and endure circles of conversations where we weren't wanted.

We've worn jeans that were so tight we had to lie on the bed just to button them. We've glued on eyelashes, and we've clipped in hair extensions. We've worn shoes that pinched our toes like they'd been rubber-banded together with a bungee cord.

We've stuffed ourselves into flesh-colored SPANX shapewear that sucked in everything below the chest all the way to our knees until we almost passed out.

We've pasted on fake smiles until our cheeks went numb, and we've sat through so much awkward small talk we've wanted to put our head through the wall. *Yes, I can clearly see that it's raining outside. Yes, I can believe it. Rain is fairly common. Please, let's talk about something that matters, for the love.*

We've done the obligatory half laughs. We've eaten food we hated, and we've tried for so long just to belong somewhere—anywhere—and now, we just want to be with people who feel comfortable. We want friendships that feel secure and safe and made to last.

We want to be known. We want to be seen. We want to be loved as we are, where we are, with what we have.

We want to be there.

But this time, we'll be wearing sweatpants.

We are so excited to take this journey with you. Together is our favorite place to be. Preferably together at a Mexican food restaurant, but this will work too.

True friendship is the destination.

Take our hands, get ready, here we go.

2

When You're Alone and
It All Kinda Sucks

love, Amy

Adult friendships are so weird.

I'm sorry, but they are.

You know it. I know it. We all know it, but for whatever reason it seems like none of us wants to come out and actually say it, so I will. Adult friendships are so weird.

I'm sure that sentence got its fair share of gasps, but it's not a bad thing to say. It's not a bad thing to think or to feel. We've been so carefully conditioned to believe we can only say nice, positive, happy things out loud, but the truth deserves to be sung from the front of the church with a full-on gospel choir backing it up.

Somewhere along the way, probably fairly early on, we began to pick up puzzle pieces that said things like:

- It would be embarrassing to admit I am lonely.
- People will always let me down, so it's better not to trust them.
- Something must be wrong with me.
- I wasn't built with that friendship button.
- Everyone already has their people.
- I am the only one who feels this way.
- It's better this way.
- If I were likable enough, I'd be able to do this on my own.

And as we've boldly laid out these pieces and tried to force them to fit together, we've found that the puzzle doesn't fit quite right. Real life doesn't look like the picture on the box. There are too many gaps, too many holes. The picture isn't clear. Some of the pieces don't seem like they belong. There are no clearly defined edges or corners. And, even worse, there are only 999 pieces in this box. (*Gets mad. Yells obscenities. Flips the entire table over and goes back to watching Netflix. Feels incredibly guilty and slightly embarrassed for the dramatic outburst and carefully puts everything right back into place.*)

Adult friendships are so weird, but let me also promise you this: just because something is weird doesn't mean it can't also be wonderful. Weird and wonderful often hold hands and coexist spectacularly in the same space.

This isn't a book filled with pretty little stories of relationships that worked out and happy endings and tales of "I thought she hated me, but it was a misunderstanding, and now we are BFFs. Haha. Isn't that the best? Hashtag blessed. Hashtag besties." (Insert eye roll here.)

Obviously, there is some of that, but more than anything, we are here to figure out what we want: a deep, lasting sisterhood with people we know and trust, who know and trust us in return. And the only way I know to help us do that is to share everything as authentically and honestly as humanly possible. The ups, the downs, the good, the bad, the things that worked out, the things that did not. The happy and a smidge of the sad too.

And to do it all with a lot of gas station snacks and old music, which make all the difference. Somebody grab me a bag of Doritos and spicy peanuts. What the heck—throw in some gummy worms too.

I once assumed certain aspects of life automatically came with being an adult: clear skin, confidence, control of your emotions, bad taste in pretty much everything, an idea of what in the world is going on, and a built-in group of friends.

I thought a crew came with the category. Like, oh—you're thirty-five? Well, things are getting real, but perk up because here are your friends! You can meet them at the local coffee shop. They're waiting for you right this moment. Yay! You will never be lonely again, and you don't even have to work to maintain these relationships because all of these people think and feel the same way you do. There will never be another Saturday night where you don't have anything to do or another party where you aren't invited. You will not be gossiped about when you're not around, and drama is—*Poof! Snap! Wink!*—a thing of the past. You're tired most of the time, and your knees hurt if you sit crisscross for too long, but you have friends—glorious friends. Now go get matching heart tattoos, take a trip to Mexico, and make everybody else jealous by blasting your photos all over Facebook.

Basically, I thought adulthood was like a Happy Meal and friends were the treat inside. I thought adult friendships would play out like a fairy tale.

But as you get older, you begin to double-think those fairy tales. Why did Belle end up with the Beast? He literally kidnapped her. Prince Charming couldn't recognize Cinderella without all the fluff? That's messed up. And Ariel's dad wasn't wrong—she was way too young to make life-altering decisions. What actually comes with being an adult is wrinkled, acne-prone, combination skin, rogue chin hairs that need to be plucked on the regular (*Why, God, why?*), a need to yell at cars driving too fast through your neighborhood, a love of folding towels neatly into thirds, no clue what's happening ever or how to fix it, possibly anxiety, and a pretty healthy dose of loneliness.

I didn't think it was possible to lose friends after the age of twenty-five. I really didn't. I thought everyone would have all the kinks worked out by then and there would be this collective consensus that we should just stick together and get along. Finding new people is exhausting. I mean, they're great, but it takes so long to break them in. They have to learn your quirks and your nuances and inside jokes, and you have to learn theirs, and it's just too much.

It's like a pair of sneakers. The new ones always rub blisters, and there's no way of knowing whether they will eventually loosen up and mold to your feet. Sure, new sneakers look good, and shopping is fun, but you have to walk a lot of miles before you get used to them. (I now understand why my dad wore the same pair of white New Balance sneakers until they had holes in the toes. I thought he was just trying to ruin my life, but nah, the man just appreciated comfy shoes.)

And then there's that stage where you've met, but now you have to use a friendship pickup line to get her number and push the relationship forward.

"So um, whaddya say me and you make a quick trip to Lululemon for some ridiculously overpriced stretchy pants? Then maybe we can hang out and eat food and I can text you a funny meme about a cat when we're done? I have Diet Coke back at my place."

I don't like it. It feels so forced and so fake.

My style is more: "Good grief, I hate boob sweat. Wanna be my friend?"

It would be so much simpler if we'd be open like that right out of the gate. We'd find the ones who understand us and like us, and that would be that. We'd sit on our front lawns together and complain about stupid meetings together, and we'd do all of life—together. Everybody would be invited. No one would be excluded. No feelings would be poked at and no needs left unmet. We'd have dinner or drinks at least once a week. And sometimes we'd fight, sure, but it would end up working itself out in some hilarious manner in thirty minutes or less.

These few sacred souls would come in and out of your

apartment unannounced, and you'd just hang out all day, every day, as if nobody ever had to work. But all the bills would get paid. Rent would be alarmingly affordable. They'd scrounge your fridge for food. You'd watch their TV. Sometimes you'd go to the coffee shop downstairs and sit on the orange vintage couch for hours listening to your one eccentric friend play the guitar and sing strange little songs, like the one about the homeless cat that smells bad.

Maybe you'd end up marrying your best friend's brother after an incredibly long, drawn-out, will-they-or-won't-they relationship. Maybe everybody's spouses would become best friends and blend into the group seamlessly. Maybe there'd be a gold swirly picture frame on the door, and maybe "I'll Be There for You" would play on repeat like the soundtrack to your lives.

Friends. That's right. I'm talking about *Friends* the TV show—Monica, Rachel, Ross, Chandler, Joey, Phoebe, all of them.

I love that sitcom, but it seriously skewed my expectations of what life as an adult would look like. I'm glad it worked out for those fictional characters, but it did not work out that way for me. Not even close. I don't even know anyone named Phoebe.

I've had a handful of best friends in my life, but things have always happened. One moved away. Actually, two moved away. That was so hard. One of them was in a completely different place in life than I was. I had a verbal fallout with one of them, and even though we tried to put things back together, the relationship never clicked quite the same again. With others, we simply grew apart for no real reason at all.

One—possibly one of my closest friends—found a new group, which broke my heart in ways I can't even begin to describe. I was happy for her happiness, but I was grieved for my own newfound loneliness.

There was never a confrontation or anything. I never understood what happened. I never will, which is the way it often seems to go. It was just a slow fizzling out of what had once been a friendship with the person I confidently put down as my emergency contact.

It started off with us simply hanging out less, which happens. Life is chaotic. Then it went from us texting two thousand times a day to us texting maybe once every other day. Then it just went awkward. It felt like she'd rather clear the friendship away completely than clear the air that stood between us, like maybe I wasn't worth the effort it would take to have a heart-to-heart.

And it's okay. She wasn't wrong. I wasn't wrong. We are different people, and we were looking for different things—but it stung. It still does sometimes. The ghosts of friendships past can haunt us long after they're over. I didn't think I'd ever lose her or that bond. I thought it was forever. Turns out we were dancing on brittle branches that were never made to hold us. They were the kind of branches that are green and full and grow in the sunshine but can't take a few raindrops without withering, going sideways, and ending up in a burn pile somewhere so kids can roast marshmallows and make s'mores.

Again, there were many tears, and there was a tremendous amount of hurt. There were nights alone in my closet after everyone else was in bed, where I would cry and pray and wonder where I went wrong. There were days where I'd remember a conversation we had and think, *Ugh, you know what you should have said? You should have said _____. Maybe that one sentence would have changed everything.* Like I said, sometimes I still reminisce and try to figure out if there was a way I could have made the final scene play out differently.

There was some passive-aggressiveness from my end because it is a language I speak fluently. Turns out, it's not healthy. Who knew? My therapist and I are working on it.

I was bent for a little while, slightly bitter, and heaven knows, my husband had to listen to me go on and on about it for months on end—bless his beautiful, patient soul. Acquaintances had to listen to it. My mom had to listen to it. My mother-in-law had to listen to it. People I didn't know had to listen to it. *God, shine down on all those precious people in a real and spectacular way. They endured so many words from my rambling mouth with so much grace and goodness. They deserve yachts, or random ten-dollar bills in their pockets. Let them wake up with clear skin, flat abs, or something equally fulfilling. Amen.*

But looking back with perfect vision, that friend breakup brought about some of the most meaningful realizations of my life. I would even go so far as to say I'm grateful for it and everything it taught me. It taught me to choose my friends wisely, to be intentional about the relationships I invest in, to guard my heart, and to go all in. It taught me to love the moment but to be aware that anything can change. It taught me to know who I am no matter what. No matter when. No matter how, and no matter who I'm around. It taught me about boundaries and learning to leave with grace. It's funny, the story reads differently when the book has been closed than it does when you're in the thick of things.

Those realizations didn't happen overnight. They didn't happen after a week or two or twenty. Learning and growth took time.

Lots and lots of time of peeling back the layers of my broken and tender heart.

The truth is, friendship is hard, and it's messy. It's messy when you aren't sure what that means for you and that other person. You aren't sure what's to come, and you aren't sure the impact it's going to have on your life. It's messy when you have to choose between settling for a friendship that's gone stagnant or sitting home alone without any plans or anyone to text. It's messy when someone you used to know like the back of your hand becomes someone you avoid at the grocery store.

It's sad when someone you relied on like a sister becomes the person you learn to only talk about the weather with because anything else could be used as a stone that comes back to strike you.

It's lonely.

It's lonely when you walk into a new place and don't recognize a single face. It's lonely when seasons end, and it's lonely when you don't even have a friend worth losing in the first place.

It's lonely when life hands you grief and you don't know where to look for solace. It's lonely when life hands you some bit of happiness and you don't have anyone willing to celebrate alongside you.

It's lonely when you are drowning in acquaintances but starving for actual connections.

I am fully human, and I have felt a wide range of emotions, but loneliness is quite possibly my least favorite of them all.

I want people to experience less of it because when people know they aren't alone, magic happens. They grow stronger, and they grow braver. They build things. They reach out their hands and help others. When people feel valued and worthy and heard, they experience extreme joy. And when even one soul experiences joy to that measure, it is like a tiny spark that becomes a flame that becomes a fire that spreads and lights up the dark places in wild ways, and I am here for it. I've always been here for it. I hope this book is that tiny spark for you, and I hope we can shine together.

⋘⋘

I love people ferociously, and yeah, I am double jointed and can bend my arms backward and that's cool, but besides that, I'm really nothing special. At the very core of me is just a simple girl who desires to be loved and to love others, and who sometimes desires to eat queso and Mexican food. That's it. I don't have a desire to become religious or rigid. Definitely not legalistic. I don't have a desire to know the most or be the most or have the most. I don't even have a desire to do the most. I love naps, Netflix, and doing absolutely nothing on my sofa too much for that. I have a heart who wants to connect with her Maker, and the more I run after him, the more I feel compelled to run after the other beautiful beings he's created. I don't know how to love God and not love people. For me, the two are bound to each other. There is no separation. God has been good to me, so I want to be good to others. No questions asked. Just really, really good.

The more I know God, the more I know my mission in life is to love people big and well and without hesitation, disqualifiers, or conditions. No hoops to jump through. So I can't let them feel lonely. I just can't.

Loneliness doesn't only affect our feelings and our minds.

It also affects our physical health in staggering ways. Loneliness is as lethal as smoking fifteen cigarettes a day.[1] *Fifteen!* Let that sink in for a moment. It reduces your immunity and increases your risk of disease. When you're lonely, things tend to magnify: stress affects you to a greater degree, financial problems take a heavier toll, marital issues seem insurmountable, health problems get worse. US Surgeon General Vivek Murthy wrote, "During my years caring for patients, the most common pathology I saw was not heart disease or diabetes; it was loneliness."[2]

I don't know about you, but when I scroll social media, or I'm out and I see a cluster of girls at a coffee shop or huddled up at a table during Bible study, my mind can spiral wildly out of control. I can quickly come to the conclusion that everyone has somebody except me. The truth is, in the last few decades, the number of Americans who believe they don't have any close friends has nearly tripled. Even sadder, according to data from the General Social Survey, when people are asked how many confidants they have, the most common answer is none.[3] In another study, nearly half of all Americans reported feeling alone at least some of the time or regularly left out.[4]

If you don't have your people yet, you're not the only one. There are more women like you than you will ever know.

There are more women without a group, without a village, without a tight team of supporters. There are more women who feel like they don't quite fit the mold, who aren't sure they have what it takes, who can't quite seem to squeeze their way into the circle.

The good news is that with so many of us craving connection, the opportunities for us to find one another are ripe for the picking.

The bad news is that too few of us are willing to plant the seeds and take the time for things to grow and flourish fully.

Friendship involves effort on both parts. On your part. On theirs. Make your peace with this truth right now or you will forever be disappointed. You will have to show up when you want to stay home. You will have to extend the invitation when you would rather receive the invitation. You will have to answer calls, respond to texts, and remember birthdays. You will have to swallow your pride sometimes, and you absolutely cannot live like you're the only one who matters, which, let's be honest, is probably good practice anyway.

You will have to understand.

I know it's hard to take a risk and raise our hands and confess to these deep-rooted feelings, but what would happen if we got brave? What would happen if we took the first step? I think we're terrified to admit, "Yeah, sometimes I get lonely" because we have this fear that it will isolate us from the crowd. But honestly, my guess is that our vulnerability would help give courage to others who are feeling the same, and we'd find we aren't so alone after all.

That's the thing about loneliness. It hurts like crazy, and it doesn't discriminate.

It is no favorer of persons. It doesn't give one tiny rat's backside whether you're famous or have a pretty face or you're successful. It doesn't care if you're rich or where you live or what kind of clothes you wear. It doesn't care about your age or your degrees or your denomination or even if you have a denomination at all. It doesn't care if you're married or single or somewhere in between. It can strike anyone at any time.

I'm always amazed at the people who confess to not having close connections with other women. *Whhhat? You're so nice. You seem like you have everything, but you're telling me that deep down you feel the same things I do? Hmm . . . seems sketchy, but okay.*

To our core, we are humans, and we are infinitely more intertwined than we care to believe. There is an unseen string running through each of us. It connects us all. Sometimes it wraps us up and pulls us close, and sometimes it's the thing that binds us and keeps our hands tied behind our backs.

We don't crave connection because we are doing life wrong. We crave connection because, to the depths of our DNA, that's how we were built. We were built to be together and to love together and to laugh together and to experience life, well, together. When those threads are interwoven with others, we all get better. Plain truth. We become better mothers and wives. We are better at our work, and suddenly, goals don't seem quite so unrealistic.

If you're feeling lonely even though you're surrounded by people, please learn to excuse yourself from tables that weren't made for you. If the table doesn't cheer when you win, it isn't the right one. If the table brushes off your struggles or ignores your pain, it isn't the right one. If they don't listen when you're trying to share your heart, you don't want to be at their table. If they're overly judgmental of you or others, always creating unnecessary drama, or don't know how to be honest with you; if they've proven repeatedly that they can't be trusted; if they aren't reciprocating the friendship—they are likely not your people.

You don't have to throw your chair back from their table or leave in a huff. Just excuse yourself peacefully. Then look for the people standing alone and build something new with them. You may have to build it with your own two calloused, cracked, unmanicured hands. Just change tables. Life is short, and it's a whole lot more miserable when you spend it in the wrong place surrounded by the wrong people, so learn to speak up. Say what you want and how you feel out loud. People can't love someone they don't know, so make yourself known.

To know true belonging requires us to be—be ourselves, be open, be free, be real. Not everyone will get it, and some people won't welcome you, but I believe that the right ones will.

If you're feeling lonely because you're actually alone, please believe that you hold the keys to unlock a whole new world of relationships.

My friend Tori asked me over for lunch one Wednesday, and we plopped our kids on the couch to watch *Toy Story 3*. I don't want to get political here, but *TS3* is the best in the franchise. We asked Tom Hanks and Tim Allen, and they both agree. (Don't fact-check this statement; just trust me.) The kids lost interest after approximately five whole seconds, but they ran around and had a blast doing whatever kids do, probably picking their noses and destroying stuff.

Tori made ham sandwiches and had a bag of chips out, and that was it. There was a laundry basket on the kitchen table, and we used paper towels for plates. It was perfect. We had never been close. We'd been friendly at one point, but that was years before, and we didn't run in the same circles anymore, so part of me was thoroughly surprised—while also thoroughly delighted—by her invitation. I asked her what made her reach out to me, and I'll never forget her answer. It was cut-and-dried and to the point, which is so Tori. "Sometimes we're the answer to our own prayers. I have been feeling lonely and sorry for myself for a long time, and finally God told me to do something about it, so I took a chance and I thought of you."

If you're lonely because you are convinced something is faulty in your makeup, please keep reading. We'll talk about this later because it deserves its own chapter, but for now: I promise, there is nothing inherently messed up with you. There may be some lies we need to detach from our brains and some falsehoods we need to shed, but you are capable of finding and making friends.

If you're lonely because you've been burned with the rays of a thousand suns and you no longer believe that people are capable of goodness, I am sorry. I am sorry for your hurt and your pain and your betrayal. I'm sorry for your bruises and your scars. I'm sorry for the bad blood. I can't do anything to erase what you've been through. I can only acknowledge that your trauma is real, and cycles are difficult to break. But please, please, please, please, please don't let one bad friendship ruin you for good. There are, what, like four billion women on this planet?

They are not all mean. They are not all catty. They are not all out there just waiting to compare and compete and bring everyone else down. Some are, and sometimes they are the loudest of the bunch, but statistically speaking, they can't all be bad.

Most women want the same things you want. They want genuine connection. They want to feel at ease and relaxed at girls' night. They want to unwind. They want to laugh. They want to hug. They want to cry. They want to be encouraged. They want to open up. They want to feel seen, and they want to be part of something bigger than themselves. They won't be perfect. Perfect people don't exist, but pretty freaking good ones do. They're out there. You can lose a lot of things, but hope isn't one of them.

What Now?

First of all, I am a homebody through and through, so I am not scared of alone time, especially if it means alone time sitting in my car in the driveway. In fact, I relish it. I'm very comfortable when it's just me. I've been hurt, and I'm terrified of rejection, but I've learned the hard way that there are two kinds of rejection: the kind that comes from others and the kind we bring on ourselves. Crabs don't eat unless they come out of their shells. Peek your head out and I bet you'll find your lobster. Step one is admitting you need friends. Step two is getting out into the world so you can find them. Here are a few ways you could do that:

- Join a gym. Listen, I've joined a lot of gyms in my day, but it turns out you have to go in order to see any physical or social results.
- Say yes when your kids' school asks for volunteers. (I know. Ugh. But just do it.)
- Find a Bible study at a local church.
- Look up activist groups, craft clubs, or start showing up to the same coffee shop repeatedly.
- Talk to other moms when you're at the park with your kids.
- Start coming out of your cubicle at work and see if anyone wants to go out for drinks and appetizers afterward. Cheese sticks are okay, I guess, but have you ever had

cheese sticks dipped in butter and breading and then deep-fried in grease? Life changing.

Go. Initiate. Invite. It is weird to introduce yourself to someone new. It is weird to make new friends. It is weird to put yourself out there, but you *are* brave. You *can* do this. You deserve this, and people deserve to know you. And who knows? You may be one conversation, one yoga class, one meeting away from finding the very friend you've been looking for. Maybe somebody is out there praying to meet you, but you'll never know if you never give it a shot.

3

WHEN YOU CAN'T AMAZON
PRIME YOUR FRIENDSHIPS

love, Jess

Recently I started Instacart, and let me tell you: I am a believer. Nothing for dinner? No problem. Someone named Sam is taking care of that for me. *No, Sam, don't bother buying those hard-as-a-rock avocados; thank you for checking. It is so helpful that you are at Ralphs testing them for me, as I am very busy wearing my house slippers right now. Also, Sam, I forgot I am actually "not at home" because I don't want to put on a bra, so please leave my groceries on the doorstep.*

There are so many cool insta-things right now, and I am here for it. Don't even get me started on Amazon Prime; Prime is like the fairy godmother I never had.

> **Me.** Fairy Primemother, I need twelve steak knives, a tutu,
> and a can opener that doesn't make me swear.
> **Fairy Primemother.** I'll have that to you in forty-eight hours.

The only problem with all these instant, don't-have-to-work-for-it conveniences is that we start to expect everything—including friendship—to be that fast and easy. We want them to show up on our front doorstep in two days, and if it takes three days, we're going to be kinda mad about it. Can you imagine if we had to go back to dial-up internet? Heaven save us; I would probably throw my computer out the window.

Despite our modern impatience, friendship doesn't work on our clocks, and it never will. There are no shortcuts to deep friendship. They take a whole lotta time and a whole lotta love.

According to research done by communication studies professor Jeffrey Hall on friendship, it takes an estimated 94 hours to make a casual friend, 164 hours to become a friend-friend, and over 200 hours to become a close friend. He said that leisure time spent together is especially important.[1]

I know that's a lot of hours, and if you're like me, you haven't washed your hair in so many days that it's starting to itch because you "don't have time." If you're like me, you haven't cleaned the cobwebs in your home since the day you moved in because of time. (That's a lie; it's because I don't want to.) We really don't have time unless we make it, but we have to make it. We. Have.

To. Make. It. Life is too beautiful and too terrible not to do it with people who truly know and love us.

Realizing you don't have friends is similar to realizing you don't have full-grown trees in your yard. You don't want a sapling. A sapling doesn't do anything. In fact, you have to water a sapling. You have to care for a sapling. You have to show up for a sapling. A sapling takes time, and you don't have time. What you really want is to be able to sit and drink lemonade in the shade of its giant branches, right this very minute. You demand the comfort only a large trunk and leaves can provide, and you don't want to wait for something to grow.

But the thing is, every single beautiful thing has a beginning. Every single friendship has to start somewhere. You can't Prime friendship, but you can start. You can start timidly and awkwardly, and someday you will be able to sit in that sapling's shade.

◄◄◄

Ten years ago I didn't have the friendships I longed for, and I knew I had to make a change. It didn't feel like something I chose; it felt like waking up one morning and realizing there was no one to call. It felt like sitting in my living room after my kids went to bed and the dark stillness suddenly seeming extra dark and extra still. It felt like turning to my husband after I turned off the TV and saying, "I'm really lonely, I need friends," and the tears falling suddenly and heavily because I didn't even know how painful their absence was until I said it out loud. That night in our dark living room, I made a very important decision: I decided to start.

The very next Sunday, I stuck out my hand to someone at

church and said, "Hi, nice to meet you. Do you want to come over for dinner on Friday?" The only confidence I had was that they would say, "No thanks, psycho, we'd rather not get murdered this week." But they shocked me; they said yes, and that's how it began.

That Friday my husband and I wished they'd said no. We prayed we would come down with some sort of illness (nothing with puking, of course, but enough to get us out of the dinner), and we cleaned our baseboards for the very first time in our entire marriage. I started cooking at eight o'clock that morning knowing I might accidentally ruin dinner two or three times, so I needed there to be enough hours left to order Papa John's. We both acted chill like we could handle it, but inside we were trying to think of any reason at all someone would want to spend their evening with us. I played out conversations in my mind:

Them. What are your hobbies?

Me. Um. Well, changing diapers, watching *The Biggest Loser*, and eating cheese, mostly. Do you like to eat cheese? Sometimes I fill a whole plate with cheddar and then I microwave it into a cheese pancake so I can eat it with a fork. How about you?

Five minutes before their expected arrival I was a mess. I was like Julia Roberts in *Runaway Bride*: *I regret to inform you that I just remembered I have somewhere to be. I'm headed to Alaska, actually; so sorry I couldn't stay for this roast I burned. Please enjoy it without me; I'll be back never!*

But we did it. They showed up, we ate food, and we thought of things to say, then the next week we did it all over again.

Sometimes it was fun; sometimes it was awkward. But all of it was freeing. It was freeing because we knew we were taking steps toward friendship, and it felt good.

And you know what? A few of those friends we invited over became best friends. The first time they sat at our table for dinner, I nearly gave myself an aneurism wondering things like whether baked potatoes were a good or bad idea. DID THEY EVEN LIKE POTATOES? While they sipped their wine, I breathed through the horrifying reality that I could see an old lipstick mark on a glass that the dishwasher had missed. These are the things you worry will make or break your friendships in the early days.

But we persisted and things got easier and easier. I even found someone who likes to melt cheese and eat it with a fork. We stopped being strangers and slowly, with lots of time, we became close friends. When they came over, I didn't worry about what I made for dinner or if I remembered to pick up my three-year-old's underwear that she loved to leave on the bathroom floor. It didn't happen with two-day shipping, but it happened, and the decision I made to invite them over and stick around for the meal was one of the best decisions I've ever made in my life.

Ten years ago, it all began, but three years ago I realized how absolutely vital each of those baby steps was. All of that watering and waiting and growing prepared me for the night none of us knew was coming.

᪵᪳᪳᪳

I heard her feet on the stairs as I was falling asleep. "It's happening; I need help," she called up with urgency in her tone. She and her husband had moved away temporarily for a job, and she'd come to visit for the week. I knew what she meant, and my heart sank as my feet hit the floor. She was in her first trimester, and she'd been having spotting for the last couple of days. We had both been nervously praying that nothing was wrong. "I'm losing the baby." I shook a little as I followed her to the bathroom. "What do I do?" she asked.

I didn't know what to do; I didn't feel qualified to be there in her pain. But I knew I belonged to that moment. I texted our other friend, "She's losing the baby," and we went to the bathroom. My friend is usually the strong one, the logical, informed one, the together one. As she sat on the toilet, she looked more fragile than I'd ever seen her.

A rush of memories came back of the day I sat on a toilet alone, afraid, and so full of death. I felt like my life would never go on and that I'd never recover. So, without thinking, I went to the tub and turned on the water. I felt the temperature with my hand until it was just right. "I'm so sorry," I said. She bit her lip and nodded as tears drained out of her eyes. "Why don't you take a bath?" I asked.

She nodded again without saying a word. I dimmed the lights and went to find candles and start a kettle of hot water. There was a quiet knock on the front door, and I opened it to find our other friend. Our eyes met, and we knew. We would do this together.

She didn't need an invitation.

She threw off her sweater and came in my small bathroom with us. "Oh, friend," she said breathlessly.

The lights were dim, the candles were lit, and worship music played softly as our dear friend delivered her baby the way she never wanted. We cried as we found the embryo. We cried as we envisioned her baby meeting their grandpa who was already in heaven waiting. We prayed and we laughed at things only three friends in grief can find funny.

We massaged her shoulders and covered them with a hot towel. We told her it wasn't always going to be like this.

That night our friendships changed forever.

This is the reason why, I thought. *The reason why we invest in one another. The reason for the dinners, the coffee dates, and the beach meetups. The reason for sharing our deep, dark secrets and the very essence of our souls.*

If she had gone through that four years earlier, I wouldn't have known how to be there—not really. Our friendship was new, like a sapling. We were still figuring each other out. When I said something off the wall, she was still learning if I was joking or serious. I was still deciding if she was the kind of person who would judge me if she knew how my house really looked before I speed cleaned it the half hour before she got there. She was quieter than me, so I was getting to know her sense of humor and how even though she dressed like a classy Nordstrom model, she couldn't wait to take off her bra (aka boob prison) when she got home. Our friendship was more fragile then; it wasn't ready for that night.

Between those early days and that day on my bathroom floor, there was a story. There were those awkward first dinners, and then there were less awkward dinners, and then there were dinners in sweatpants, laughing until we peed a little. There were walks and there was wine on the dock while we watched the sunset. There was running errands at Target; there was doing our

Costco Christmas shopping. There were brunches at our houses that ended up lasting most of the day. There was CATAN, and there was a spring break road trip to the sunshine that ended in a snowstorm. There were a million texts, and there was throwing each other's baby showers.

There was a whole lot of learning that we didn't have to pretend around each other. There was a lot of telling truths like "Today is hard, I'm struggling" instead of "I'm doing great! How are you?" And then there was a lot of learning that the other person was a safe place for that much truth.

Sister, believe me, I've been the girl looking out the window at an empty front yard. I've been the girl miscarrying with no one to call who I felt *that* comfortable with. I've been the one who all of a sudden woke up and found herself without the close friends I longed for. I'd grown up, friends had moved away, we'd started our families, and suddenly, I was without. I've been the one looking across the fence at someone else's yard full of large trees and wondering how the heck they were so lucky.

Now I know it wasn't luck; it was time.

<hr />

Yesterday, my friend's rainbow baby had her second birthday. She is fire with a side of fire, and I absolutely adore her. Her name means "full of life," and she is. She squealed with delight when we all sang to her, then we laughed because you cannot be unaffected by her joy.

The story continues. The story now includes a miscarriage, a move apart, and a move back. It includes my friend showing up at my house with a baked chicken and sweet potatoes when I was sick. It includes lots of prayer and phone calls when she was sick. It includes me helping her pack her clothes and telling her it was definitely time to let go of that pile of dresses from college. It includes more babies born. It includes strolling Target and requests like "Hey, can you grab me a bag of onions when you go to Costco?" It includes "that hurt my feelings" and heartfelt apologies and a bazillion more texts about anything and everything. It includes taking our kids to the zoo, and it includes holiday meals spent at the same table, feeling grateful for each other.

It's not that our friendship never had challenges or conflict; it had both of those things. It's just mature. It's a full-grown tree in my yard, and it keeps getting bigger. We can drink our lemonade beneath its branches because we've done the work. We can enjoy the shade, and we can laugh at our inside jokes because we've invested in our friendship tirelessly. When things have been hard, we haven't disappeared because we both cherish this beautiful thing we've built.

The other night she and I were having drinks with a couple of girlfriends. We were talking about marriage, and she told us how her husband had casually mentioned that he thought it was nice how I always kept my house so clean. We all laughed hysterically because they know how far from the truth that is. I'm a great rage cleaner when I have people over for dinner, but if you stop by my house on a Tuesday you're going to low-key wonder if there are any adults who live in this home, or if it's entirely run by children. It's okay, I wonder that too. Also, children are disgusting. I said what I said.

My friend shared that since she has been staying home from

work with her kids, her husband was hoping the house would be "as clean" as mine. He's not a chauvinist, by the way. If the roles were reversed, he would expect the same (and then his expectation would be lit on fire as all stay-at-home parents are painfully aware).

The next day she texted me, "Hey, I'm at your house. Can I grab my sweater?"

"Oh shoot," I said. "Yeah. I just ran to the coffee shop, but the door is unlocked."

"Okay," she said.

A few minutes later I received a picture of my sink overflowing with dishes and a box of Cheerios spilled next to it. "I'm taking pictures for my husband," she said. "That okay?"

"Bahaha. OF COURSE."

The goal is to be real. I have no desire to be anything else with my friends. The goal is to build friendships that can withstand walking into the mess without fear or judgment. And maybe the goal is to have each other's backs, even when having each other's backs means exposing your kitchen to outside scrutiny in all its midweek glory.

⟞⟞⟞

Plant the tree, sister. Don't wait another day. Starting is always the most overwhelming part, but it will get easier. I've been there, and I'm telling you: it's possible. Don't overthink it; just do it. Invite someone over for an awkward first dinner. If that doesn't work out, invite someone else. Keep inviting; keep watering; keep investing.

If I could go back to talk to that girl sitting on her living room floor with tears streaming down her face, I would take her hands in mine and say, "I'm so, so sorry you're lonely. I know what that feels like, and I know it hurts deeply. Listen, there is nothing wrong with you. You're not broken or unlovable. You're not a unique case that is destined to be without good friends. There is hope. If you plant the seeds, you will reap the fruit. With a little bit of courage and belief in yourself, you can do it. I know you can do it."

I want you to start small with something that feels manageable but also pushes you out of your comfort zone. Talk to someone new, invite someone over. At first it will feel awkward. Don't worry if it does (it's just part of the process). It's going to require a little bit of courage and a whole lot of consistency. Treat friendship like you're going to the gym for the very first time. It doesn't matter that you can't do it that well or that it makes you really, really sore; that's just part of the process. The important thing is to keep showing up. Soon it will get easier.

Eventually your efforts are going to lead you to connection. Once you find connection, keep investing in that friendship. Keep loving and pursuing and watering.

You're going to find friendship. You're going to find the kind of friendships that you long for. It's going to be a process, but the process will be joyful (mostly), and the payoff will be irreplaceable.

I want you to know there is hope. So, so, so much hope.

If you're lonely today, if you're looking out at your front yard and it looks barren and dry, know that it's very possible there's only a hundred hours between you and your next best friend. It's very possible that there are just a few stories between you and a full-grown tree.

What Now?

- Write down one or two things you're going to do every week (or month) to grow new friendships or care for the ones you already have.
- Text your friends every Monday to check in on them.
- Make a standing date for girls' night, like Tuesday happy hour or wine at someone's house.
- Have a monthly casual friend-dinner night and make it a potluck with paper plates.
- Once a week do something special and out of the norm for a friend (buy them a coffee, send them flowers).
- Strike up a conversation with someone new at least once a week.
- Call or FaceTime a friend who's far away every Thursday.

It doesn't matter what steps you take—make them personal to you and your lifestyle. Remember, baby steps are just the right speed for success. You want to make sure you're giving yourself manageable, bite-size goals so you can stick with them.

Deep friendships don't come with two-day shipping, but the truly important things in life never do. Keep investing, my friend. Keep watering. Keep loving. Keep being reliable and consistent. It will be worth it. So, so worth it.

4

WHEN INSECURITY
REIGNS SUPREME

love, Amy

Sometimes, I do a fairly decent job of faking confidence.

"Amy, I love that you are exactly who you are. You don't care what anyone thinks. You're so brave."

Ummm. Let's get two things straight here. I care what literally everyone thinks, and I second-guess myself every waking minute of the day. And sometimes in my sleep, but okay.

Nine times out of ten, if you give me a compliment you'll get to watch me squirm like—I don't know—something squirmy.

A worm? I will immediately respond with a laundry list of my less-than-desired qualities.

Anyone. Amy, you look pretty today.
Me. Oh, you're so nice. No. Um . . . I uh . . . this shirt
is new, but I didn't brush my teeth this morning, and
my leg hair is half an inch long. It's a real cactus-like
situation I've got going on from the knee down. Do you
want to feel my kneecaps for proof?
Anyone. Nope. I'm good, but thanks.

Awkward, but I do it almost every single time. It's instinctual at this point.

Somebody builds you up. You aren't accustomed to being put on a pedestal, so you tear yourself down a notch or two and end up back on the ground rolling around in the dirt right where you believe you belong.

It's not a wonderful quality. Yes, obviously insecurity isn't great, but this manifestation of it also takes away from the kind individual who just said the nice thing about you. And taking away from them can inadvertently take away from the rapport they were attempting to establish with you. They were trying to give you the gift of kind words, and by putting yourself down, you basically threw that gift right back in their face. Please stop doing this. Just say thank you and continue to move the conversation forward. Don't undermine their compliment and don't discourage them from handing out words of admiration to others.

I know we aren't always used to believing nice things about ourselves, but accept the love when it comes from someone else.

I am also an unrelenting people pleaser. More on that next. Honestly, it requires an entire chapter. Maybe an entire book. I could fill some pages. PLEASE JUST LIKE ME.

I don't stand up for myself. I say yes when I want to say no. I become furious within if I disagree with anyone, so I typically stay away from voicing my opinion because otherwise I will lie awake for hours rerunning the conversation through my head. Plus, who even cares what I have to say? I travel in the direction of the flow even when I feel the flow is doing it wrong. I fish for compliments. I hate that one. I can be overly defensive. I basically assume everyone is mad at me all the time. If you're going to be my friend, I'm going to need you to text me here and there with a random "Hey, Ames, just letting you know I'm not mad at you. Okay, love you. Bye."

I could literally be handing out warm, gooey, delicious chocolate chip cookies, and in my head, I'd still be thinking, *I hope these don't taste like burned pieces of Play-Doh and baking soda. I hope they don't make anyone sick. OH MY GOSH, THE SALMONELLA. These chocolate chip cookies were a bad idea.*

Listen. Chocolate chip cookies are never a bad idea. Bless my poor brain for having to process all this junk. There truly is no rest for the insecure.

Do you know which insecure habit of mine throws people off the most?

I talk. I talk a lot.

I talk a lot no matter what. Possibly because I'm an only child, so I never had anyone to talk to or play with growing up. Instead it's like I banked all of those words into my system, and they are just now coming out in adulthood. Or maybe I just had no annoyed sibling around to tell me to shut up. I dunno, but I know it's worse when I'm nervous and when I feel like I need to prove myself. When that social anxiety kicks in—whew. What comes off as confidence to others feels to me like internal energy ready to spontaneously combust.

I have no problem speaking, so I'm usually okay at parties. Some might even describe me as "a hoot." I'm loud, I'm funny, and I'm perky. I get excited easily. I dance. I sing. I make jokes, so many jokes. People are always baffled when they get to know me and my insecurity reveals itself.

The thing is, even though it seems like words are what's flowing, it's really fear. Fear of rejection. Fear of being left out. Fear of being unliked. Fear of saying the wrong thing. Fear of offending someone. Fear of being gossiped about. Fear that I'll be accepted at first and then pushed to the side later. Fear of being boring. Fear that I'm not good enough—not good enough to be at the party, not good enough to have as a friend, not good enough for anything really. Fear that I'm wearing the wrong thing or doing the wrong thing with my hands. *Am I swinging them the right amount? Am I using them enough? Too much? Hands in my pockets? Oh, for the love, I'm not even wearing pockets. Why do they even make dresses without pockets?! Do I clasp them together? Put them on my belly. No, that's strange. On my hips? Do they always just dangle like this? They just . . . they just hang there.*

I'm also prone to compare. Every chance I get. I think everybody else is doing it better, going further, and overall running laps around me in life. And if I struggled with comparison before, let me tell you, Instagram hasn't made it any easier.

I think, in general, I have wasted a good portion of my life doing some combination of the following three things:

1. Wishing I were somebody else
2. Mimicking someone else
3. Believing I was okay, but only on the stipulation that someone else approved of me

My husband and I try to be somewhat regular with date nights. Keyword here is *try*. Are we always successful? No. No, we absolutely are not, but date nights are important to both of us, so we give it our best. Anyway, this one night, we were on our way home from an actual rodeo, because Texas, and we noticed this long line of cars at a dead stop ahead. We could see cop cars, flashing lights, and mild chaos, but we still couldn't figure out why everything was so backed up.

Lanes were open. Nothing major seemed to be happening, but nobody was moving an inch. We sat there for forty minutes in our stupid boots and cowboy hats desperately wanting to get home.

Turns out, there had been a teeny-tiny fender bender earlier. There wasn't anything to see, so why the traffic? Everyone could have just driven through like normal.

And then I noticed something—every driver had been moving slowly so they could look over and see what was going on. You know how people are: we're nosy. We want the lowdown. We want to know what's happening over there so we can compare that experience to what's going on over here. And the more attention these drivers paid to somebody else, the less they were able to focus on the road directly in front of their faces.

It's kind of what we do as humans.

We let somebody else's successes or somebody else's failures stop us from seeing the road laid out before us. We let somebody else's beauty put a dim light on the mirror we are looking into. We let whatever is going on with them bring out a lot of discontentment in our own lives. We get jealous. We get guilty. We get puffed up. We get deflated. We get proud. We get petty. We get down. We stop looking at our own lanes.

And sure, comparison may be the thief of joy, but it's also a solid first step toward insecurity, and insecurity is the thief of pretty much everything else.

In fact, I think I could fix at least half of my problems if I could overcome my insecurity. Possibly more.

Insecurity will wreak havoc on your mental health, your work, your goals. It will sneak in there and mess up your marriage, your relationships, the way you see yourself in the mirror, the way you sleep. You'll stop seeing yourself as someone who was created with a purpose, and you'll start seeing nothing but a mess. It will deflate your ego, your drive. It will either make you work and work and work—as if all that hustle could somehow make you more worthy—or it will make you roll your eyes, rip your dreams into tiny shreds, and say, "What's even the point?"

A dirty view will make everything around you appear dirty too.

It will make you desperate, and nothing will destroy a good friendship quite like desperation. People love a friend who shows up. A friend who is consistent. A friend who isn't flaky—because while flaky is a wonderful quality in a biscuit, it's a horrible quality in a friend. People want a friend who is reliable and readily available. But a clingy friend? That's a whole other story. Sometimes friends need space and a little room to breathe. Sometimes friends need to know you are self-reliant and self-assured enough to handle things on your own. They want to be there for you, but they don't want to be your sole source of satisfaction and happiness. That's too much pressure to put on any one person. It's not fair to them, and it's not fair to you either.

Somehow, we believed—at least I did—the vicious lie that insecurity and humility have the same blood running through their veins. But that's completely wrong. Insecurity does not equal humility. The two are not friends. They don't even hold hands, go to the same school, or live in the same town. They don't know each other. Insecurity will keep you looking inward until you become blind to others. Humility simply recognizes that you aren't better than anyone around you, and you've all been cut from the same beautiful cloth. Humility is insistent on finding the good in other people. Insecurity is insistent on finding the bad in us.

Insecurity forces us to focus fully on ourselves. Humility has this wonderful way of forcing us to focus on others.

It makes us want to know them. It makes us want to know who they are and what makes them tick and to celebrate their beauty. It doesn't mean we're going to get along, agree, or be best friends. It just means we know the same God who is able to love us, loves them equally. No better, no worse. He looks at his children with the same degree of care and affection. Insecurity will make us work *for* love instead of *from* love. There is only one letter of difference between the two, but believe me, the variance here is massive.

When you work for love, life becomes a game, and not the fun kind like charades. Actually, I kind of hate charades. Too much pressure, too much spotlight. Spades. Spades is a fun game.

Working for love is exhausting to the bone, through and through. I can't think of anything that will leave us high, dry, empty, and brokenhearted quite like this hustle.

We can spend our entire lives, every waking hour, trying to build our houses on insecurity, but those houses are going to come crashing down over and over again. They were laid on a cracked foundation. The bones are weak. The walls are made of sand. They can't hold up through a storm.

You'll be strong when they love you. You'll be weak when you're no longer their favorite. You'll be high when they choose you. You'll be low when you don't get their invitation. You'll be steady when they understand you. You'll be shaky like an old car the second they question you.

You will take your worth and put it in somebody else's hands, and off the top of my head, I can't think of a less secure place for your worth to be held.

God did not create you, craft you, and carefully plan out each line on the palm of your hand so you could shut down and hide away because you got rejected. God did not put all that wonderful work into you so you could walk away and decide you weren't good enough. God did not meticulously make you so you could criticize, tear down, and condemn every single one of your quirks. And they are indeed quirks, not flaws.

Cars have design flaws. Clothes, shoes, and purses have design flaws—pieces of the fabric that weren't sewn together quite right. Bicycles have design flaws. Phones have so many design flaws that I often want to scream. Anything made by people has design flaws. Anything made by God is flawless. Wonderful, good, and beautiful. You're a reflection of him.

You're not perfect, but how bad can something made in his image really be? Seriously.

You can believe God is good, or you can believe he messed up when he made you, but you can't do both. Take your pick.

⟨⟨⟨⟨⟩

A few years ago, before I was ever writing or blogging, I gave birth to my third child, a baby girl. Around late December or early January, I vividly remember sitting in a recliner, rocking back and forth, nursing her while bawling my eyes out as I wrote my New Year's resolutions:

- Lose the baby weight.
- Stop talking so much.
- Read more.
- Get organized.
- Be a better mom.
- Tone it down.
- Learn new recipes.
- Stop failing at everything.
- Don't be so you.
- Try to make some friends.
- Try to keep those friends. Don't screw it up like you normally do.
- People obviously don't like you, so change.

New Year's resolutions are fine as long as you're doing them for the right reasons, but like so many of us, I was doing them because

I couldn't stand who I was. I was doing them because I was broken and a little empty and looking for something. Also probably because of all the hormones and postpartum stuff. But being hard on myself was nothing new. I've been this way my whole life, and it's never worked in my favor. In fact, I can't think of a single time being hard on myself has benefited me or the people around me. I can't think of a single time that it's built me up or gotten me closer to the person I want to be.

Something came over me. There I was, holding this precious girl who was going to be watching everything I was doing. She was going to speak about herself the same way I spoke about myself. She was going to look at herself the way I looked at myself. If I didn't like my thighs, she was probably going to believe something was wrong with hers, too, and if I talked about my weight constantly, it was likely going to become a fixation for her as well. So I knew right then: it had to stop. Self-criticism had run through the women in my family for generations, and it would continue to do so until somebody had the nerve to knock it down. That somebody was going to be me.

That generational curse had met its match, and I wasn't falling for its crap and its lies and its disappointment anymore.

So I ripped up my list, and I made an un-resolution right there on that chair. I wasn't going to change myself. I wasn't going to count my calories for a week and then sneak a few slices of pizza during family movie night, talk about how guilty I felt for indulging on those magnificent carbohydrates, and give up. I wasn't going to walk around tearing myself down. I already knew my faults. I mean, trust me, I'm aware of everything wrong with me. I didn't really need them spelled out.

This was going to be the year I accepted myself. I was going to do it for me. I was going to do it for the three kids in my house who watched my every move, and I was going to use this confidence to glorify God because my insecurity sure wasn't a testament to his goodness. I was going to raise my hands in the air and say, "Here I am, God. Use me."

For a year, I dug deep. I figured out my personality. I went to therapy. I tried to understand what my patterns were and unlock all of my strengths. I took control of the things I could change and released the things I couldn't. I tried to be a little more self-aware and a little less self-conscious. I found freedom and gave myself permission to just be.

It was like cuddling up on the warmest couch I'd ever known.

And in the process, something miraculous happened: my relationships blossomed. I loved my husband a little more. The energy in the house was a little lighter. There were more smiles; there was more dancing. We took more pictures and arranged more playdates. I started inviting people into my world exactly as it was, which was new for me.

Before when I'd have people over, I would go all out to impress them. I was so sure that if my house could be the cleanest or my food could be the yummiest or my games could be the most fun, I could prove my worth as a host and as a friend. One time, before hosting a night of Bunco, I was so nervous that I stayed up all night repainting my kitchen cabinets. It was insane of me, because (1) I don't even know how to paint kitchen cabinets, (2) I need sleep—I am a bear without at least seven hours, and (3) the right people don't care about the color of your cabinets; they care about the way you make them feel. But I was so insecure that I searched for anything to settle my anxiety. For whatever reason, cabinets were it that time.

I don't change my house anymore when I'm having people over. I mean, I pick up the dirty socks and underwear, and I spray some Febreze in the bathroom, because with three boys that place tends to smell like a dumpster mixed with dog urine, but no more painting the cabinets at five in the morning. Now I just focus on welcoming people into a house that feels comfortable and worn in, like an old sweater. If they're my friends, they won't mind. If my house isn't good enough, well then, I've just learned that they aren't my people, and even that is a gift of sorts.

I have to assume this awakening was because I finally wasn't trying so hard. I had welcomed myself. I had honored who God made me to be, and this gave me the energy I needed to breathe more life into the people around me. I relaxed, which meant I was easy to relax around. I was honest for maybe the first time in my entire life. Everything was more fun. My feelings weren't being hurt on a regular basis. I could brush off minor setbacks. I could stop being passive-aggressive and acting like some wounded animal. I didn't see things as a personal attack against me. If you did not like me or wave me over to sit in your circle, it was okay because I believed someone eventually would. I stopped needing so much from other people. I stopped relying on their affirmations, their approval, and their invitations and started giving those things to others instead. If you haven't yet discovered this yourself, let me tell you: giving is pretty great.

I don't know if this makes sense, but it's as if I liked myself enough to get over myself, and when I got over myself, it allowed me to focus on everyone around me, which is the single largest key to connection.

Insecurity makes you walk into a room and suddenly become acutely aware of everything wrong with you. Insecurity is a nit-picker of who you are, what you look like, and what you have.

Why did I wear this? I look stupid. I'm walking weird. Is my voice high? All of a sudden my voice is so high. WHAT IS GOING ON WITH ME? Say something clever. Say something funny. Make everyone laugh. Make everyone like you. Nope, don't say that. That was dumb. Take it back. Take it back. Take it back.

Confidence, on the other hand, makes you walk into a room and become acutely aware of what everyone else is doing right. You say things like "You look so beautiful" and "Your shoes are amazing" and "You raise some interesting points, that is so clever" and "I could talk to you for hours."

You listen to every word *others* have to say because you aren't all up in your own head thinking about yourself or trying to craft a response. It's about them. Not you.

Boom.

That's the key to friendship: to make people feel liked. To make it about them, and to care about their feelings and their needs.

It's a hard thing to do when insecurity is oozing out of your pores, but it becomes natural when you are laced with confidence. Everyone wants to feel good about themselves. Everyone wants to feel accepted, seen, and heard. Everyone wants to feel loved, and it becomes exponentially easier to love others, and love others well, when you are more at ease with yourself.

As a whole, women have this horrible habit of getting in

groups and bashing ourselves, especially when it comes to our appearances. Like that scene in *Mean Girls* where Regina George is all, "My pores are huge," and Cady Heron responds, "I have really bad breath in the morning."[1] I've been to girls' nights like this. Heck, I've actively participated in girls' nights like this.

"Oh no, I'm just going to get a salad. My thighs are stuck together like plastic produce bags at the grocery store, and they jiggle like a bowl of banana pudding when I walk."

"Yeah, I have to do something about the lines on my forehead. They've gotten so bad."

We go around the table, taking turns, hurling insults at ourselves. We pretend like being awful to ourselves is a normal, playful activity. This is just what women do. Our grandmothers did it. Our mothers did it. It is a rite of passage. We laugh in the moment, but deep down, our tender hearts shed a tear or two because words matter. They really do bring life or death—to our dreams, our joy, our confidence. We all leave worse off than when we arrived. We may think we're only putting ourselves down, but in reality, we are putting down every single woman at the table.

I'm never self-conscious about my gray hairs unless I'm around another woman who is self-conscious about hers. I'm most aware of the pooch hanging over my jeans when I'm around another woman who is aware of the pooch hanging over her jeans. There's nothing—nothing—that makes me want to cling to my cellulite quite like somebody else clinging to hers.

And if someone smaller than me refers to herself as fat or says she needs to lose weight—oh, the pain.

If confidence is contagious, then surely insecurity is too.

There is a distinct difference between being vulnerable with your struggles to a trusted source, between laughing at your unwashed hair with a friend and dogging on yourself in a negative way. There's nothing fashionable about hating yourself, and there's nothing favorable about purposely putting yourself down.

⠀⠀᚜᚜᚜⠀⠀

After one particularly rough girls' night where the self-bashing seemed to be at an all-time high, I flung the back door open and threw myself dramatically on the couch next to my husband, where he very lovingly asked, "You have fun?"

"*Nope.*" I exhaled. "Not really fun at all, and I'm starving."

"What? Why?" he asked, genuinely surprised.

"Well, for starters, every single person was doing something called the keto diet. Nobody ate the birthday cake, and I didn't want to be the only one eating, so it just sat there, taunting me, looking all delicious and stuff. It had buttercream icing, Brandon! *Buttercream!* Everybody just kept harping on how ugly they were, and I think they're beautiful. Those are some of the most gorgeous women I know. And if they think they're ugly, good grief, what do they think about me, ya know?"

"No, not really, but I'm sorry."

"It's okay. It's not your fault. I just didn't have much to say. Plus, I really wanted some of that cake. I may go buy myself one tomorrow just because I can."

I need more substance in my food, and I need more substance in my conversations.

To my fellow friends struggling with the beast of insecurity: it's okay. An appearance-obsessed culture has brought us here. Filtered images on Instagram have pushed us to this place. The dangerous lie that lives inside the walls of so many churches that insecurity is synonymous with humility has led us to this barren land. Generations of women criticizing themselves have pulled this out of us, and some of this, quite frankly, we have very much done to ourselves.

Insecurity is a sneaky, nasty little monster of a thing that slithers its voice into our everyday thoughts. It's a creature that burrows its way into how we think about ourselves—our bodies, our personalities, our ability to achieve, our intelligence, and our roles as mothers, wives, partners, and friends. It's a tool the devil's been throwing at women for a long, long time, but thank goodness, it's one we can fight. We are not powerless to the lies, and we are not powerless to the voices.

One of the greatest things we will ever learn in this life is to tell these voices to shut up.

Ugh, okay. You again. The Insecurity Jerk. Bug off. Get out. Offense intended—you do nothing for me, and also, you suck. I will not be negotiating with you today as I am both busy and exhausted, and that's the end of it. Move along, you giant germ. I have work to do and people to love. You deserve none of my focus, but they do. Those people out there deserve the best of me. Booyah. (Do people still say *booyah*? They should. They really should. Do you hear that, everyone? We're bringing *booyah* back!)

Sometimes, I think we have repeated these denigrations over and over to ourselves so many times that we have accepted them as fact. We have unknowingly welcomed them into our hearts as true and sound and solid logic. They are not. The only way I know to dismantle these lies and shake off this coat of criticisms we've sewn for ourselves is to notice when the lies creep into our thoughts, interrupt them, and replace them with little pieces of encouragement. That critical coat is not doing anything to keep you warm. It is, in fact, the reason you feel cold and empty and exhausted.

Change your social media feed. If you've filled it up with influencers who make you compare your life to others', question yourself, and believe that you can't be whole unless you fit into the right jeans, own a designer belt, and live in a spotless house—unfollow. If the people you've surrounded yourself with don't talk about anything deeper than the way they look or the things they own and it's bumming you out—change the conversation at the table or change the people you're sitting with. If you're stuck in a cycle of dragging yourself down—stop. Stop right now. If the way you feel about yourself goes up and down with the number on the scale—toss the scale in the trash.

Your weight changes. Your face ages. But your heart doesn't.

If talking bad about yourself can become a habit, then so can speaking life.

If you believe your value comes solely from the acceptance others give you—get to know yourself a little better. Better yet, ask God what he thinks about you. Ask him who he thinks you are. He's gonna say good things. Read the Psalms and Song of Songs. Repeat David's words: "I am fearfully and wonderfully made" (Psalm 139:14). Get the kind of confidence that only comes from above. God made you. God knows you better than anyone, and he's a fan.

Insecurity keeps us shackled to comfort, and comfort keeps

us forever shackled to conformity, and conformity keeps us forever shackled to the things of this world.

But when you find confidence, pleasing people becomes less important than pleasing God. Fitting in becomes less important than standing out. Working for love becomes less important than working from a place where you know you are loved and where you know you have plenty of love to give to everyone you meet. We can stop living like we're empty. We're not. We're full. We're full of God's love—more than we will ever know. We are his handiwork, and that's something.

In confidence, you become your truest self, and this is essential to every good friendship. As you find your most authentic self, you'll find your most authentic relationships. No, not everyone will like you, but the ones who do will love you fiercely. No, not everyone will accept you, but the ones who do will embrace you with open arms. No, not everyone will invite you, but the ones who do will want you in a way that makes you feel seen and known and valued. No, not everyone will want you, but the ones who do will hold on to you loyally, and you won't have to paint your kitchen cabinets every time they come over. You can just shove the laundry off the couch and make a seat for them.

You are loved.

Get out there. Stand tall, and act like it.

What Now?

Empowerment comes through knowledge, so get to know yourself. Here are some ways you can start:

- Find a personality assessment that works for you and take it. There are plenty out there: the Enneagram, Myers-Briggs Type Indicator, DISC.
- Discover your spiritual gift.
- Make lists of your strengths and find ways to use them to help others. I will *always* believe that helping others is key to a good life.
- Own your faults and hone them too. We have to know who we are, and we have to work on who we aren't.
- See a counselor. Get a therapist. Have a professional guide you. This is what they've been trained to do, and honestly, they're amazing. We don't have to be struggling with anxiety or depression to see a licensed doctor. We don't have to be in the pit of despair, barely holding on, to get help. We need to normalize regular emotional upkeep. It's a lot easier to keep up with oil changes than it is to buy a completely new engine.
- Learn to interrupt your negative thoughts. This one is hard, but it is possible. I once kept a notepad with me and wrote down all of the negative things I said to myself throughout the day. It was alarming to see them all spelled out, to say the least. By ten in the morning I had said some of the cruelest, nastiest things to myself. Things like:
  - Wow. You look awful this morning.
  - You're late again because you're failing.
  - You're messing up your kids because you can't get it together.
  - You will never have good friends.
  - Your hair is so thin.
  - Your skin looks so blotchy.

- You aren't as pretty as you used to be.
- You will never be successful. It's kind of stupid that
  you're even trying. You look like a fool.

I'd spoken to myself in a way I would never dare speak to a friend—or even an enemy. When I could see all the hurt and damage I was doing to my own psyche, I knew I had to change. I don't even know how I was getting through my days after mentally ripping myself to shreds, and I don't know why I thought this was acceptable behavior. It's not. It's not acceptable. It's not okay. But before I could change, I had to admit that there was a problem. Little by little, I learned (and am currently learning—it's a process) to recognize my negative self-talk and replace it with something kinder and gentler.

Write a self-affirming letter. Memorize it. Take it to heart. Repeat it before you walk into a social event if you need to. Repeat it anytime your heart needs a boost. Here is mine if it helps:

Dear Amy,

There is nothing wrong with you.

You have been uniquely designed and perfectly planned. You are a daughter of the King, and no part of you is an accident. You're good enough, and you were made for right here, right now. You were made to do these things and to say these things. You can go confidently because you don't go alone. You go with him.

Keep your heart open. Keep being good to others. Live fierce and love free.

Believe. Breathe. And have a good time.

5

WHEN YOU'RE PRETTY SURE
YOU'VE BEEN DUPED

love, Jess

I've always been pretty gullible. It's one of my husband's favorite qualities about me because if he teases me, there is a 95 percent chance I'll fall for it. That has continued to add excitement to our decade and a half of marriage.

Husband. (says any bizarre thing that pops into his head)
Me. What?! Are you serious?

Husband. (doesn't break eye contact, but eyes start to twinkle)

Me. Oh haha.

Husband. (feels proud of himself for years to come)

When I was ten years old, I had a best friend who made life like a movie. His imagination was a whirlwind of fairy tales, magic, and mischief. Everything was bigger than life with him. If we walked by a horse in a pasture, he'd tell a story about how the horse had been stolen by a rodeo clown and sold for glue. If we played in the woods, he'd tell me he could see fairies in the trees and bear prints in our fort.

One day we were out exploring when he dared me to taste a plant he'd pulled out of the ground. "It's really good for you," he said. "You're not scared, are you?" He took a big bite and grinned at me while he chewed it.

Scared was the very worst insult. I glared at him. "I'm *not* scared." I didn't break eye contact as I ate the plant. After I'd swallowed it, his eyes got big. "I accidentally gave you the wrong plant," he said, feigning horror. "That's the one that's poisonous."

"Yeah right," I said, used to his tall tales. "Anyway, you ate it too."

"I've spent years building up immunity," he explained sadly.

At that exact moment his mom called for him to get in the car. I stood there, frozen, with the plant hanging limply from my hand while he raced up the hillside to meet her.

"I don't believe you!" I shouted.

"See ya!" he called over his shoulder.

"I don't believe you!"

I spent the rest of the evening spitting. I spit as I walked to the house and then I sat on the porch and spit some more. I figured this might be my last day on earth, and spitting was my best chance at survival. My mom came out to ask me why I was salivating all over her flower beds. I explained my dilemma and the corners of her mouth quivered.

"Which plant?" she asked. I showed her and she laughed. "You're fine, hon, he was teasing you. Those are just carrot greens."

Well played, buddy, well played. Next time you tell me you found Jesus' tomb at summer camp, I'm on to you.

Except I wasn't.

I'm pretty much the same way as an adult. Like, I kinda know certain things aren't true, but also, buckle me up and take me for a ride because maybe you're right. I'll roll my eyes on the outside but probably spend the next five hours spitting (just in case).

I don't know about you, but I feel like we've been told a whole lot of lies and tall tales about friendship, and I think I fell for most of them. For a lot of my life, I lived by that book of "truths" that turned out to be a book of lies (brought to you by insecurity, teenage movies, and bad advice). Like I said, I'm gullible. I have fallen for a lot of harmful lies, ones that threatened to truly destroy me—and I'm not just talking about that brief period in my early twenties where I believed wearing gaucho pants with sparkles was a good idea. I'm talking about lies that kept me imprisoned and stuck. Lies that kept me isolated and alone. Lies that sucked the life right out of me.

That plant didn't end up being poisonous, but a lot of the lies I believed most definitely were. Now that I know the truth, I want to sing it from the rooftops. If you have believed any of these lies or still live under them, let's kick them to the curb one by one.

Lie #1: We Have to Be Impressive to Have Friends

We've been fed this one since junior high. *If I'm pretty enough, skinny enough, athletic enough, funny enough, then I'll be accepted. If I'm enough, I'll belong. If I'm enough, I'll be loved. If I'm enough, I'll have friends. If I'm enough, I'll be invited.* Pieces of our souls die under that kind of pressure. If you were like me, you kinda knew that all of the things riding on these "enoughs" were hollow and untrue, but you also spent hours in front of the mirror and all your money from your job at Dairy Queen on Abercrombie & Fitch graphic tees (just in case). If I was lonely, I assumed it was because I needed to get red streaks in my hair (which I did) or visit the tanning bed and get little heart stickers on my midriff (which I also did). Push-up bras and Lucky Brand jeans were my teenage version of watering the flower bed with saliva.

As an adult, I still find myself staring into the mirror and using far too much brainpower worrying about the quarantine pounds clinging to my thighs and underarms. Yeah, it's annoying when my pants don't button, but there's something deeper there, and I still struggle to remember that my size has nothing to do with my value.

We've grown up, but some of those beliefs have dug in deep. Listen friend: the endeavor to be enough is a big lie. I know it and you know it, so tell that voice to take a hike. You are enough as you are, and so am I. We don't need to be prettier, smaller, stronger, or anything other than as we are. It's just carrot greens, my friend; you're okay.

Lie #2: Popularity = Connection

We've traded the halls of our middle schools for scrolling squares and the world of likes and follows. Instagram, Facebook, TikTok, and all the other new social media platforms I'm too uncool to know about have changed the game. The thing is, popularity (still) has absolutely nothing to do with friendship. I don't care how many followers you have; that ain't never gonna lead to connection. Not if you have one hundred followers, one thousand followers, or one million followers. Have you ever listened to Justin Bieber's song "Lonely"? If not, do yourself a favor and listen to it now. Some of the lyrics go, "What if you had it all / But nobody to call?"[1] Those words make my soul ache because they're so true. So many of us live under the delusion that popularity will fill the void in our hearts. Friendship is friendship. Popularity will never be the same thing (ever). We can have a billion people admire us, but that will never fill the same need as having even just one person truly love us. If Bieber Fever isn't cutting it, it's safe to say no amount of popularity will.

Lie #3: You Must Filter Your Mess out of the Picture

This is a new one (I think). It's come right along with Snapseed and Lightbox and the Portrait mode on my iPhone. I'll be honest—I love to brighten my pictures. (Crow's-feet, begone! I shall stay in denial of you forever along with everyone who doesn't see me in real life.) Filters are God's gift to tired moms whose dark under eye circles have taken over. Did I get punched repeatedly in the face? No, that's just how I look now. I have kids. Thank you for understanding.

I'm definitely not against filters.

It's just important to remember when to stop filtering. You can't only give a pretty version of yourself to your friends and expect to be truly connected. You have to let yourself be truly seen. You can only be loved as much as you're known. I like seeing brightly lit photos of design influencers I follow, but I *love* being invited into a house where there's a laundry pile on the couch. Friendship is about real, no-filter-needed life.

Lie #4: Friends Should Understand When You Go MIA

This lie also applies to when you never text back, never show up, or are too busy to get together. I see memes all the time that say things like "You have to understand I might not ever text you back, but I still love you" or "I want to be invited—I just won't ever come." I get it; life is crazy, and there are real things that keep us from being able to be there sometimes. I've had seasons of dark postpartum depression when I was completely unable to pursue my friendships. There are all kinds of things that can come up like that, and if that's where you're at, this is not for you.

The thing is, being a bad friend can be situational, but we shouldn't turn it into a lifestyle. At that point, it's just an excuse.

Good friendships take intentionality; you can't ignore them and expect them to be healthy. You can't cancel last minute, can't never text back, and you can't be a bad friend and expect to have good friendships. You just can't. You can't take and take and take. You can't treat people like you don't value them and then expect them to value you. It's just not the way it works. If you're always too busy for your friends, you will have shallow friendships.

Being an absent friend and having good friendships isn't a thing.

Lie #5: It's All About Self-Care

Self-care *is* important, and we need to hear that because often women suck at self-care. A massage, exercising, lone trips to Target (or if you're a mom, lone trips to the shower), having boundaries—all those things are valuable. When we fly, we're told to put on our own oxygen masks before we assist anyone else. Take. Care. Of. Yourself. (Louder for the people in the back.)

But, as Amy always likes to say: once you've got on your oxygen mask, turn to your friends and help them with theirs too. If you only prioritize you, you'll be very lonely once you reach your destination. Loving and serving go hand in hand, and we can't forget that deep friendships require that we give of ourselves and that we love and serve our friends, sometimes sacrificially. That means showing up (even when you don't feel like it), pursuing, bringing a meal when they're sick, and not being a fair-weather friend.

Lie #6: Friendship Is an Extra, Not a Necessity

We've treated friendship like a luxury for far too long. Friendship isn't a luxury; it's essential. We need people. We need connection. We need to belong. It even affects our life expectancy. In my opinion, that means we don't wait to invest in it "when we have time"; it means we invest in it now because it's a really, really big deal. I think subconsciously we have friendship far down our mental checklists. It needs to be near the top—not lost after busy schedules, soccer practice, and chores. Those things are important, but they're not more important than having close connections in your life.

We don't just want it; we need it.

Lie #7: Friendship Is Impossible

Most of us have been hurt and disappointed in our friendships, and sometimes, in order to protect our broken hearts, we buy into the narrative that friendship is just too good to be true. *People don't have good friends as adults; that's just how it is.* No matter how true this one feels, please don't buy into it. Good, deep friendship is possible, and it's entirely accessible. It may take some hard work and determination, but this book is a road map that we pray will help take you there.

Lie #8: Friendship Just "Happens"

We often wait for friends to just show up in our lives—kinda like a rom com, but for pals: girl is just doing her thing; everyone else has friends except for her; she is so sad and does not know what to do; she walks in the mall and collides with the most perfect potential friend ever; potential friend picks up her shopping bags; and when their eyes connect, they realize this is fate. They go straight to Cinnabon and discover in two minutes of conversation that they both love caramel lattes and long walks in Target; they exchange Insta handles and vow to watch *The Great British Baking Show* together; and they live happily ever after. The end.

The thing is, friendship rarely goes like that. We often have to be intentional and pursue the friendships for which we are looking.

This narrative that it just "happens" takes the power right out of your hands and gives it to an invisible force. The truth is, you have the power. Maybe you're waiting for someone to notice you, but so is everyone else.

It's time to take the power back.

Lie #9: Saying "Bye, Girl" Is the Norm

Friendship isn't always easy or smooth sailing. Don't hear me wrong on this, but we can throw around the word *toxic* kinda loosely. There are toxic people, and there are people it's appropriate to "cancel." But that's not all people. It's probably not even most people.

Most people are good people who have flaws. Hi, hello, one of those people is me. We need to be willing to fight for our friends even when our feelings are hurt. We need to fight for our friends when the going gets tough and there are misunderstandings. Things aren't always smooth—that's normal. Be careful not to look for reasons to move on.

We need to love others fiercely, just like we need to be loved fiercely.

Lie #10: You're the Only One Without Good Friends

Everyone is basically hanging out all the time without you. That's how the narrative reads. Everyone else buys matching shirts and goes on vacation together. Everyone else has friends who care enough to check in. Everyone else has friends who remember their birthdays. Everyone else has friends to double date with. Everyone else has friends to _____.

Nope. Just nope.

I know it can feel that way, and it's true some people have amazing friendships. But let's set the record straight about "everyone." Three in five Americans report being lonely.[2] That's more than half, and that's definitely not everyone. Even if someone is currently connected, I would bet my right leg that they've felt like an outsider at some point in their life. I'd bet that they've felt that sickening pang of loneliness just like you have.

You are not alone. You're not the only one (read and reread). We are, in fact, on this journey together, so let's link arms and do this thing. A better future awaits.

⟫⟫⟫

When I was dating my husband, Graham, we talked a lot about getting married. I told him that it was probably impossible for him to surprise me with a proposal because my spidey sense was very good, and I was sure something would give him away. A few days before our second dating-anniversary, he sat me down at the coffee shop where I worked. He struggled to get the words out, "Babe, I know we want to get married this year, but I'm just not financially there yet. I need time to save, and I don't want you to be disappointed that it's probably not going to happen for a while." My heart dropped to the pit of my stomach. I have a lot of gifts, but patience is not one of them. I cried, and I told him I understood. He looked so sad and said, "I just didn't want you to think it was coming with our anniversary."

"Oh, I didn't," I lied. I was so disappointed, but I did my best to hide it.

The next day was my day off, and he asked me if I wanted to help him with something. A friend of ours wanted to surprise his wife for her birthday and wondered if we'd set up a picnic for them at a mountain lake nearby. "Yeah sure," I said, "sounds fun."

We swung by our friend's office, and he gave us the picnic basket and blanket. Our friend was a hopeless romantic, and absolutely everything he did was over the top. He had roses and a gift for his wife and instructed us to hide a video camera. We listened to the new Weezer album as we drove to the mountains. It was winter, and the snow was deep, but the sun had come out and melted the pebble-covered beach. "I have no clue where to set this up—where do you think?" Graham asked.

We found a pretty spot, and I laid out the blanket and started getting food out. He took a couple roses and ripped off the petals to spread them around. "What are you doing?!" I shrieked. "They probably wanted to keep those!"

"I don't know," he said with a shrug. "I thought it would

look cool." I started to have a mild anxiety attack thinking about the mutilated bouquet. Our friend was very particular with his vision. "It's fine," Graham said, laughing at me. He hid the video camera and checked his watch. "Thirty minutes till they get here," he said. "Might as well hang out for a bit."

The lake was glassy and reflected every mountain ridge and peak. "We should see what he got her," he said about the present our friend had sent. It was covered in embroidered butterflies—an homage to his nickname for her.

"Um no," I said.

"Why not?" he pushed. "I just want to see."

"I don't! What if they walk up!"

"They won't," he coaxed. "Come on."

He started opening the box. Riding on the horror of the mutilated bouquet, I begged him to stop, convinced they were about to round the corner.

"Come on." He laughed. "Look at this."

I peeked hesitantly in the box, and there lay a bright-red thong. On the front was a flame with the words "Wild Thing" in yellow. "*Yuuuckkkk*," I shrieked. "I *never* needed to see that!"

"Let's see what's under it," he said.

"*No!*" I shouted, terrified at what we might find. "They're going to be here any second. *Stop!*"

He tossed the thong to the side and started opening a jewelry box. "*Stop!*" I begged again, but it was too late. Inside was a white-gold ring with a sapphire. My first thought was that it was strange our friend was buying his wife a second ring, and then I looked up to find Graham on one knee.

I never saw it coming.

It's crazy, I know, I know, but I told you: it's easy to pull a fast one on me.

My favorite part of the story is that Graham had asked his mom to get something to cover the ring box that would throw me off, and she'd chosen a red thong from the dollar store. That right there is why my MIL wins at life.

We've been sold a lot of half-truths and straight-up lies when it comes to friendship, but the good news is that the truth is even better than we expected. It's a whole lot like a sapphire ring hidden beneath some cheap underwear. The truth is what we've actually been longing for all along.

The truth, my friend, is that you are enough exactly as you are. The truth is that friendship is not a popularity contest (thank God). The truth is that investing in your friendships is worthwhile and it matters a whole lot. The truth is, you don't have to wait for a friend to magically pop into your life. There are tools to go out and find them (read: you have the power). The truth is, we're all in this boat together, and you're not alone. We've all been lonely; we've all been disconnected.

So let's link arms and take this journey together.

The friendships we long for aren't impossible to find; they're actually very close by. Maybe they're right around the corner.

What Now?

Grab a notebook and jot down some lies you've believed about friendship (maybe they're in this chapter, maybe they're not). Circle the one that has made you feel the most defeated and stuck.

Now write a letter to yourself with the truth. Dig deep and write with the kind of compassion you would use when writing to your little sister, your grandmother, or your daughter. I'll start with the letter I wish I had written myself ten years ago:

Dear Jess,

I know you often feel like you're not enough. I know you often believe the lie that you aren't lovable as you are (with all your flaws, all your failures, and also your cankles that have been passed down in the family for generations). But you are enough. You are beautiful. You are loved. You are worthy. As. You. Are. The end.

I'm going to say something to you that you really need to hear: stop trying so hard. Stop trying to reach an impossible standard. Stop spending all your money at that expensive store in the mall. Take all that attention you're focusing inward and focus it outward. Pursue someone who needs a friend. Encourage someone. Turn your attention to love someone else as is. Doing so will empower you to love yourself as is too.

You've got this, you really do. Also cankles are kind of cute.

Love,

Jess

Ten Qualities in a Really Good Friend

1. *They can be real.* Fake is exhausting and overrated. We're all kind of a mess. Friendship is a whole lot better when you can be in the mess together. Authenticity adds a beautiful level of depth and understanding to the relationship.

2. *They are a safe place for you to be real.* Dirty yoga pants, bad nights, fights with the hubby, trouble with parenting, depression, anxiety, heartburn from eating too many tacos—whatever it is you're bringing to the table, you want friends who can handle the real you. If you can't ever relax when you're around them, they're not your home.

3. *They make time.* Everyone is busy, but if you want true friendship, you've gotta carve out the time consistently. Consistency is key here. It's important you have friends who will do that whenever they get the chance, even if it's squeezing in a ten-minute phone conversation while they're going through the car wash or sending a quick text at some point in the day. If you never see or talk to them, it's hard to know them. And if you never know them, it's hard to build a relationship with them. In fact, it's kind of impossible.

4. *They like you for YOU.* Listen, and listen real good. If you have to impress, perform, or work hard to keep them around—stop it this second. If they don't love you when you stop, then *get out.* Ain't no one got time for that. Your energy is better spent where it is valued.

5. *You can trust them.* You know your words stop with them; they have your back when you're in the room and when you walk away.

6. *They're approachable.* It's never fun to let a friend know they hurt your feelings, but it has to happen sometimes. Friends who listen, really hear you, and can apologize are so precious.

7. *They show up.* Birthdays, bouts with anxiety, grief, good times, bad times, celebrations—friends who show up when it matters leave lasting impressions.

8. *They aren't super-duper negative.* There's a difference between being honest about the ups and downs of life and spewing a fire hose of negativity constantly. You should feel good around them the majority of the time.

9. *They're an all-around good human.* Just like your mama said, you've gotta watch who gets your attention. If they're nice to you, then turn around and act like a jerk to the waitress— they're not nice. Friends should make you want to be a better human, and they should see the value in others.

10. *They pursue you right back.* It's essential to find friends who check in, invite you out, and text first. They initiate. They invest. They pursue. Relationships and bridges—neither of 'em work if they only go one way.

6

WHEN YOU WONDER WHY
NO ONE LIKES YOU

love, Amy

There is this girl I know who doesn't like me.

I've tried. Truly. I've dropped off homemade chocolate chip cookies on her doorstep. I've invited her places. I've made it a point to compliment her when we see each other. "Oh my gosh, I love your top. You look gorgeous in purple. It really does something with your eyes. *Blah blah blah.*"

But still, I can feel her distaste for me—possibly because I'm being slightly fake and trying way too hard. I'm being nice, darn it. Please reciprocate and give me fake compliments in return. Isn't that the way the world is supposed to work? Ugh. It drives me crazy.

I can sense her desire to run in the complete opposite direction whenever she sees me, and I can tell her entire being wants to moonwalk out of any conversation we have, but for whatever reason, I still want to grab her by the sleeve and force her to stay so she can finally understand how great I am.

I have absolutely no idea why she doesn't like me. I have rewound every single scenario, and I have run through every single thing I could have possibly done to offend, annoy, or hurt her at least one million times over the past few years, and every single time I come up empty. That's not true. I am perky, and I can come across as "a lot" most of the time. I get nervous and I talk too much half the time, and then the other half I get nervous and I don't talk at all. I confuse myself, so the annoying thing—I get that. But every single time I get out my magnifying glass and little brush and start dusting and searching for clues as to the moment things went awry, I find no fingerprints, no mess, no leads. Nothing. I'm quirky, sure, and I'm awkward, but I am likable, darn it.

I have wrestled with this, and I have beat myself up with this over and over and over. It has kept me up at night just like those greasy breadsticks from Domino's I continue to eat, even though I know the food is going to be tearing up my esophagus at three o'clock in the freaking morning.

And then a few months ago, do you know what I found out?

It was all in my head.

I'd made the whole thing up.

She was crazy about me. Big fan. Big. Huge.

Nah, I'm just kidding. I found out she, indeed, does not like me at all.

You thought this was ending differently, didn't you? Nope. I wish that were the case, but this isn't one of those cutesy we-actually-became-best-friends-oh-my-goodness Disney Channel misunderstandings. Those stories are sweet, but that's not the way it always goes. Sometimes, the story goes sour. My feelings have misled me more times than I can count, and heaven knows, I am prone to get carried away and fixate on the dramatic—just not this time. This time I was spot on.

I think we all have our big "thing." You know, something we struggle with on a deep, deep level. It's almost as if these struggles are woven into the very fabric of who we are as human beings. We can't remember how the thing got there, and even with counseling, self-awareness, book reading, and all the motivational quotes in the world—it remains.

My thing is people pleasing.

For some, it's perfectionism. For others, it's control or jumping to the worst-case scenario. Then there's the desire to show off and the need to be more successful than anyone else. It's almost like we're all out here trying to prove something to the world. We're all out here fighting for our worth—to earn some kind of elusive trophy to place on top of the mantel, brilliant with shine and distinction, that says, "Here. Look at this. I did it! I matter, world. Take that. I won the gold, and here it is in all its glory."

I think I matter most when I'm liked. In fact, I think I only matter when I'm liked.

I always picture life as this race. We're all out here jogging/

running/walking/sprinting around this track—trying to get to the finish line still standing. Meanwhile, Satan is doing everything he can to stop us from reaching the white tape at the end. (Is the tape white at the end of a race? I don't run, like, ever, so I have no clue. Maybe it's yellow?) He's out there hiding in the bushes, and every once in a while he throws out a stumbling block. Sometimes, it's something major. Sometimes it's something minor. It can be anger, jealousy, pride, insecurity, talking badly about people, staying silent when you should speak up, speaking up when you should stay silent—literally anything.

Sometimes when he throws a block out, we hop right over it—barely even giving acknowledgment to its existence. Other times, we fall flat on our faces. Every time, Satan takes note.

Oh, that one got her. That's the one. I'm just gonna keep it here in my back pocket for next time. Oh man, I'm Satan, I don't have pockets, or the need for pants at all . . . but I'm gonna remember. This is the one that gets her.

Can't you just hear his maniacal laugh?

If Satan can get me believing that somebody doesn't like me, I've disappointed someone, or someone is mad at me, I will quickly become obsessed, fixated, and even controlled by that belief. I will be putty in his nasty little devil hands, and I will allow him to mold me into the absolute worst version of myself.

As I'm writing this, I realize how ridiculously trite that must sound to you. I am indeed a full thirty-seven years old, not twelve, and last I heard, there are something like seven billion people on this planet. Of course they don't all like me. That's asinine. To even begin to think it's possible would make me wild with delusion, but still. There is something somewhere inside of me that whispers, *If they don't like you, it's because you're doing it wrong. You're the problem. Fix yourself, girlfriend, for the love. Measure up.*

If you're a fellow pleaser, you get it. You're probably nodding along right now, or you have a few tears welling up in your eyes that you're trying to blink back because you've been working your entire life to earn that nonexistent trophy too. For a lot of women, it's how we've been raised. We've been taught to be good, sit still, and be pretty. To keep our mouths shut. Never to rock the boat. To change our style, our clothes, and everything about our appearance to fit in. *Make your eyebrows thinner. No! Not that thin! What have you done, become Gwen Stefani from the nineties? They'll never grow back. Aah. Now get them microbladed onto your face permanently. But make sure they look natural, even though they're completely fake.* That's the key, isn't it? To be fake but look natural. It's exhausting.

The amount of energy it takes to read a person and go, "Okay, this is what they expect of me," then be that? To feel like you're only enough if you can somehow miraculously manage to mold, melt, and twist yourself to fit others' expectations? To be everything to everyone at all times? Whoosh. It makes you lose a little piece of yourself. It makes you push down who you really are and go silent about all the things you really want to say. It makes you forget the million little pieces that have gone into building you into the woman you're supposed to be. It's like handcuffing yourself to everyone else's opinion of what makes you worthy.

I like to believe that one day, I'll wake up and just not care what anyone thinks about me anymore. I'll be that old lady with pink hair and giant bedazzled sunglasses who dances in the middle of the grocery store because Justin Bieber came on, and I'll be bold, and I'll be brilliant, and I won't mind so much if someone thinks I'm wrong or doesn't like what I have to say. I won't mind if my opinions are offensive to someone. (PS: Your opinions will always be offensive to someone. I once had a follower go off on me because I said I didn't like avocados, which is an opinion I stand by. They're expensive, finicky, and mushy. You may have all the guacamole; just leave me the queso. Green mush is a no from me.) I won't stay up and wonder why I wasn't invited, and I won't try so hard to go with the flow. I'll learn that there is a distinct difference between keeping peace and creating peace, and I'll discover that conflict isn't the end of the world; it's just a part of life.

But until that happens, there are a few things I can do.

First, I can recognize my desire to please people. You can't change something unless you admit it exists. So what are the signs of being a perpetual people pleaser? For me, these can include:

- Constantly agreeing with everyone.
- Apologizing for things that aren't my fault.
- Being so easygoing that I never have an opinion.
- Saying I'm fine when I'm actually upset.
- Avoiding all confrontations and shying away from serious conversations.
- Thinking everything is a personal criticism.
- Having trouble making a decision without asking people what they think first.
- Never being proud of myself until other people applaud me.
- Offering to do things even though I truly don't have time to do them.

- Signing up for things I don't actually want to do.
- Struggling with boundaries and saying no.
- Finding it almost impossible to be assertive.
- Believing other people's feelings are solely my responsibility.
- Rarely standing up for myself.
- Allowing myself to be taken advantage of on a regular basis.
- Feeling terrified that having needs will make me a burden to others.
- Getting mad at myself for having feelings that aren't always positive.
- Believing I can only be a good friend if I am perfect and exactly who the other person wants me to be.
- Being unable to find a sense of peace when someone doesn't like me.
- Feeling like I'd rather be unknown than unliked.

If I catch myself thinking or doing any of these things, I know I'm in a bad place and need to reset my thoughts and behaviors.

Second, I can work with my desire to please people because it isn't all bad. Just like almost every personality quality, there is a head and there is a tail. There is a good and there is a bad. It is the best part of me, and it is the worst. It helps me take others' feelings into account. It keeps me focused on their needs. It makes me slow—very, very slow—to anger. It anchors me to peace. When used correctly, these are wonderful traits.

And, finally, I can fight the desire to let my people pleasing tendencies completely control me and every decision that I make.

Zero out of five stars to that—do not recommend. I'd rather lose the people who don't genuinely love me than lose myself trying to make them all happy.

People pleasing is a game that can never be won. It's a prize that can never be found, and there is no contentment to be found when you live your life searching for something that simply doesn't exist.

⋘

A few years ago, I had a simple revelation. My dad was in the thick of a battle with kidney disease—the same thing that killed his dad, my Poppy, right before I was born. My dad was on dialysis, both of his kidneys had been removed, and he was waiting and hoping for a transplant, not knowing whether one would ever be available. My heart crumbles for anyone with a loved one waiting for a transplant. The process is grueling and gut-wrenching in every way imaginable. I was coming to terms with possibly losing the man who raised me, while being tested for kidney disease myself. I was grappling with life and death. I was begging God to hear my prayers, and I was feeling like they were bouncing off the clouds right back to the ground where I was lying in a muddled heap. It wasn't exactly the happiest time of my life.

This may sound pretty dark for a book that is meant to be a fun, light read, but stick with me for a moment. I was in a season where the fragility of life was all too clear for me, and I began to wonder what people would say about me after I was gone. Would they say I was kind? Would they say that I'd lived for Jesus? Would they say I'd given it all to his glory? Would they say I was inspiring and courageous? Would they say I'd lived abundantly? Or would they say I was always worried about what other people thought? Would they say I wasted most of the precious time God gave me because I was consumed with the desire to earn others' approval? Would they say I'd lived with freedom and abandon, or would they say I'd always been a shell of a girl who desperately wanted to fit in?

Because I did desperately want to fit in. I did desperately want to please people. Up to that point, being liked was the driving force in almost every decision I made, every word I said, and even the way I cut my hair.

If I wasn't enough for others, then I wasn't enough. Period. People pleasing wasn't something I did; it was something I worshiped. It wasn't just how I lived; it was why I lived.

I kept picturing the kind of eulogies people would give at my funeral and the stories they'd tell, and I had visions of them saying things like "She was nice. She was a good girl. There really wasn't that much else to her. She spent a lot of time caring about what everyone else thought. I don't know if she ever really lived or if she only existed for their recognition. She sure did like to be liked, that Amy."

In the middle of these storms, while wrestling with my worth and wondering if it would ever be possible for me to cut ties with my lifelong addiction to people pleasing, I took my kids out for some fine dining on waffle fries and chicken nuggets. I looked around, and it was like a bolt of lightning hit me: I can't be everyone's Chick-fil-A sauce. And that one, simple sentence—those six little words—changed everything for me. Let me explain.

I was sitting at Chick-fil-A while my kids were running in and out of the play place, begging me for ice cream and tattling on each other to no end, when I noticed something I'd never given much thought to before. On one woman's tray, I saw ketchup and ranch. At another table, I saw packets of barbecue, Polynesian, and honey mustard sauce. I had chosen Chick-fil-A sauce myself because let's be serious—it's the best one. It's utterly bizarre to me that anyone would want anything else, but that's the thing: people aren't the same.

Everyone chooses differently. Everyone's needs vary. Everyone's wants fluctuate. Everyone brings different things to the table, and everyone expects to take different things away. Nobody is the same. Nobody prioritizes in an identical manner, and there is no one standard to what makes a person a good friend, so I probably shouldn't take it so personally when someone doesn't like me, when someone doesn't want to be my bestie, when I feel left out or excluded. I mean, I can't be everyone's Chick-fil-A sauce, and neither can you.

For some people, you are going to be too salty, and for others, you're going to be too sweet. For some, you will be too bold, and for others, you won't have nearly enough flavor. You will be both too much and not enough for some people's taste buds, and that's okay.

God didn't make you to be loved by everyone. He didn't make you to be generic and bland. He did not send you to this earth so that you could be invited to all the parties or included in every group text. He did not carefully form you and make you and meticulously count the number of hairs on your head so that you could be popular or please all the people. He made you to love him and to follow him and to carry out his very specific purpose by being your very distinct flavor.

Your flavor won't be for everyone. It's essential that you accept this, move on, and start walking in confidence like a woman who has been set free.

The next time the devil tries to attack you or make you crumble over the vicious lie that something is inherently wrong with who you are because you are feeling rejected, alone, or picked over; the next time Satan tries to get you so fixated on being liked that you forget the battle has already been won; the next time you begin to pile all that pressure on yourself; and the next time you begin to believe that the prize is some nonexistent trophy, remember to come up for air and breathe.

None of that is from God. The Enemy is trying to get you so entangled in your own self-doubt that you shut up and stay home. He's trying to keep you so exhausted with the stress of maintaining the status quo that you don't have anything left to give back to God. So your focus will shift from pleasing God to pleasing people.

You can't be everyone's Chick-fil-A sauce. That's not your job. Your job is to run the race that's been set out before you. Run it hard. Run it long. Run it well. Run it in your very own style.

Run with arms wide open toward faith and hope. Give grace. Chase after gratitude. Bring joy with you everywhere you go. Do what God's asked you to do and keep your eyes on him. Be encouraging and kind and open. Keep fighting whatever your "thing" is. You might not wake up and instantly be cured, but take little steps every single day to get closer to where you want to be and then breathe. A pure heart won't be enough for everyone, but it'll be enough in the end.

And just in case you were wondering, my dad got his kidney. He retired from his job, started a new company, and traveled to places like Israel, Hawaii, and a handful of other American states with his wife. I'd say he's doing just fine, and we are thankful for the gift of more time with him every single day. Also, as for now, my kidneys are clear too. So yay!

※◆※~

It took me a while, and it's something I'm still learning. Appeasing everyone by being a watered-down version of yourself is, in fact, not the best way to keep friendships alive. It's a good way to hit it off with people initially, sure, so I understand its appeal. But to maintain a healthy friendship, the other person has to know you—all of you. They deserve to know your ins and your outs, your weird little wirings. They deserve to know your opinions and your insights and your beliefs. All of those feelings and ideas and passions you keep buried down—give them a voice. Let them be heard, not so you can drown out anyone else but so you can give them existence.

People can never know you if you don't know yourself, and you'll never know yourself if you constantly change to keep up with whatever version you feel forced into this week.

I'm terrified of being kicked out of every group, and I'm scared of being alone. I worry that when someone doesn't like me, it's because I'm a bad person who has gotten it all wrong. I convince myself that the only way for me to love people is to earn their stamp of approval.

Wrong.

Sometimes people just don't like other people for no real reason at all. Oil and water. You could run yourself absolutely ragged trying to figure it out, but what a sad way to spend your life.

I see your pain, and I empathize with your fears because I, too, have them. But the kind of vulnerability that makes it possible for people to reject you is the same kind of vulnerability that makes it possible for people to love you.

I promise, there are women out there who will accept you exactly as you are. They'll want you, and they'll welcome you, and they'll give you a safe space. It won't happen often, and it won't happen with everyone, but the ones who choose you will choose you fully. The ones who genuinely love you won't yank that love away the second you disagree. A friendship that is right isn't delicate, and it can handle you being yourself. In fact, it hangs on you being yourself, and it can only come alive when you give it the kind of oxygen that comes from being authentic.

What Now?

Embrace yourself and embrace your unique flavor.

Stop assuming everyone doesn't like you and start assuming they do. Walk into rooms with your head held high. We all ignorantly believe that the key to having friendships is to be liked, when in reality, the key to having friendships is focusing less on ourselves and more on others. Instead of trying to make people like you, flip the script, and make people feel liked. Compliment them. Encourage them. Listen well. Seriously, learning to listen will grow the ways you're able to connect with others like nothing else. In general, people like to talk about themselves. This takes some of the pressure off you, and it makes them come alive.

Here are a few reminders. Highlight them. Memorize them. Scribble them down on a sticky note and put them somewhere you're sure to see them:

The right people will accept you because you are yourself, not in spite of it. The right people will love you because of your passions, your ideas, and your opinions, not in spite of them. The right people will never mind being told no every once in a while because they will genuinely want you to be happy. The right people will yearn to know you in a substantial and meaningful way, and they will never know you if you never unshackle yourself from your need to please people all the time.

If you want to be a good friend, you have to live with freedom. Everyone won't like you. It isn't something you can manipulate or control, so instead of trying to control somebody else's emotions toward you, control what you put out there. Make sure it's a lot of love and a lot of good, then rest easy, friend. You did what you could, and that will always be enough.

7

WHEN FAKE MAKES YOU
WANT TO HURL

love, Jess

I cannot with decaf coffee. I know a lot of you enjoy it, but maybe some of you have learned to live with it. I'm not trying to disrespect your choices, but I do not like coffee that pretends to be coffee. I don't mean to brag, but I can call out a fake in under ten seconds. (Takes sip. *Nope, I still have zero desire to put on pants or change the world, and the heart palpitations are also missing.*) You cannot sneak one by this girl. Don't be coming at me with your big ole cup of steaming sadness. My entire personality depends on the real deal.

You know what else I need to be real, and real only? My friendships. I'd rather singe my own eyebrows than be stuck for a long time in surface-level conversation. Sometimes when I get trapped in conversations about the weather and Meghan Markle's housing situation, I have an out-of-body experience where I look down on our exchange and wish for the Lord to return for his bride.

Listen, I can hold my own in the coffee line and with strangers at the bank. I like shootin' the breeze with those people, mostly because lines are boring, so my expectations are not that high. They probably don't want to know that I am having a bad day because I'm having cramps, anyway. But if I'm hanging out with my friends, I don't want to be stuck in the shallow end of the pool. Don't get me wrong, snort laughing about our sex lives also counts. I'm not saying everything needs to be all deep and heavy; I'm saying I want to take off every mask and every filter and just be.

I want to be real with my friends, and I want them to be real with me too.

Friendship should be the place that we walk into with our bare feet and our favorite sweatpants. It should be the place where we lay it all out and nothing stays hidden. It should be the place where we come as we are and snuggle up on the corner of the couch and share our dreams, our fears, our joys, and our struggles. It should be the place where we're known and loved and given the benefit of the doubt. It should be the place where we are safe to just be. It should be the place where we can eat thousands of calories worth of brownies and ice cream. It should be the place where we can vent without being judged. It should be the place where we can ugly cry and snort laugh. It should be the place where we feel absolute belonging.

The sad thing is that most of us have experienced the exact opposite of that. We've experienced cattiness in high school bathrooms. We've experienced being left out because we didn't wear the right brand of jeans or know how to do our makeup. We've experienced conversations that revolved around nothing but gossip and negativity that left us feeling like we were never going to be enough, no matter how hard we tried. We've experienced feeling like we had to take small bites of our food because everyone else at the table was dieting. We've experienced being ghosted and not included. We've experienced thoughts like *I can tell they don't like me but I'm not sure why.* We've experienced holding in our tears.

We've experienced friendship being a stage on which to perform instead of a safe place in which to belong. It has been the opposite of comfortable. It's been the opposite of belonging. It's been restricting and ill fitting, like wearing a bra with an underwire while you're eating Thanksgiving dinner. We kept coming back because we longed so deeply for connection, and every time it dug in and didn't feel right, we assumed the problem was with us. We've thought, *Is this just how it is?*

Deep down, though, we know there's something better.

Before I go on, can I say something? I'm sorry that you had those experiences. I'm sorry for each and every time you've felt lonely in a room full of people. I'm sorry for each and every time you've felt unworthy in your friendships. That's not how friendship is supposed to be; it's not. Friendship should feel like coming home, not like tiptoeing around in a glass castle.

Listen friend: that come-as-you-are kind of friendship is rare, but it doesn't have to be.

I moved a lot as a kid, and every time I moved, it felt like tryouts for friendship. I went into overdrive trying to figure out who I needed to be at this school to be accepted. All I wanted was to belong, but I forgot myself in order to do it. I strove to say the right things, to wear the right things, and to be interested in the right things. At one school, I wore wide-legged pants and oversized T-shirts. At the next school, I slathered on green-and-blue eyeshadow, tried my hand at cakey foundation, wore bootcut jeans, and put star stickers at the corners of my eyes. At the next school, I spent all of my money on T-shirts that said Abercrombie, got skater shoes, and put red streaks in my hair. I think some of that was me, but it was only the version of me that I thought was acceptable.

I will never forget being in a room full of people and still feeling desperately alone. I will never forget surveying the lunch-room only to be consumed with panic that I didn't belong and there was no place where I felt invited to sit. I will never forget sneaking past the hallway monitors just so I could lock myself in a bathroom stall until the lunch period was over.

As an adult, things didn't feel much different. I wasn't walking fluorescent-lit halls anymore, but I was still trying to walk through early marriage, through new motherhood, and through learning to be an adult.

It was different, but it was the same.

Sometimes our pain shows us exactly the kind of table we

want to build and exactly the kind of friend we want to be; I know it did for me.

Friendship shouldn't feel like squeezing into your skinny jeans. There shouldn't be any groaning and heaving while you lie on your bed and force the last button through the button-hole. Friendship should feel like "I'll be there, but I'll be wearing sweatpants."

Friendship can be a sacred place if we let down our guard, let each other in (like really in), and let ourselves be known and seen. In that space, insecurity disappears if we set a precedent for each other that you belong here, no matter what.

◄◄◄◄◄

One time, I went to a skin care party. The evening was led by a woman whose skin looked like she dined on magical flowers and dragon's blood. She showed us sample after sample of things we "must have" to appear younger. She even did some lotion voodoo on a woman by tightening up the skin by one of her eyes so that she looked like one of those before-and-after meth posters, except the woman would have to pay $299 to un-meth her other eye.

Anyway, I was just trying to find room in the budget for lattes, so gold-encrusted skin care was not in the cards for me. Also, there were not nearly enough snacks at this thing, and someone had forgotten to bring wine.

At one point, the presenter said we were going to play a "fun little game" called "find out how old your skin is." She passed out notebook paper and pens. "Write down your age, and now add seventeen years if you've ever (even once) been in a tanning bed.

Now add ten years if you've ever stepped foot outside of your house into actual sunlight. If you drink seventeen glasses of water a day, you may subtract two months from your age," and so on. Well, when your skin turns out to be seventy-two even though you are, in fact, still twenty-eight, it is not a "fun little game." Apparently my three visits to the tanning salon in 2002 made me ready for a senior discount. God forbid I'd ever smoked a single cigarette or inhaled the scent of a margarita.

Anyway, I was not in a happy mood by the time this thing wrapped up. I was hungry, broke, seventy-two-years old, and I was ready to go home. Then the presenter remembered she had one more thing to show us.

Freckle removal cream.

And that is when I peaced out to go eat brownies and drink wine in the privacy of my own home. Just me, my seventy-two-year-old skin, and my freckles.

When I burst through my door all ragey, my husband was like "What's wrong?"

And I was like "Well, I just found out my skin is geriatric, for starters, and also I'm going to need like a thousand dollars for some serums, or there is no hope."

He looked at me with a quiver in the corner of his mouth and a spark in his eye.

"*And* I just found out that freckles are a 'blemish' and that people pay big money to get rid of them!" I was angrily letting the red wine glug unclassily into my Kerr jar.

That is when the quiver could not be contained, and he burst out laughing. He was dying. "Your skin is seventy-two?" Actual tears formed in the corners of his eyes as he struggled to breathe.

"Yes. And I'm sorry that I'm going to be 250 by the time I die because I like the sun."

"Babe." He gasped for air. "Your skin is not seventy-two, and I love your freckles." He could barely get the words out before he was howling again.

The truth is, I have laugh lines because I've laughed a lot. I have forehead lines probably because of my high school vanity problem and a deep desire to be the color of my Hawaiian Tropic tanning oil. But the freckles? Don't even get me started on the freckles. Those are here to stay.

I'm not against skin cream. (I am against parties without snacks.) I'm not against getting rid of your freckles or dropping a wad of cash on magical creams. I'm really not. I'm just against the pressure to be someone you're not, especially in friendship.

I'm against walking into a room feeling fine and leaving thinking you need to fix everything about you to belong.

I'm against the pressure to conform, the pressure to fit in, and the pressure to be a certain way. Real, deep friendships require that we show up as our real, deep selves. Sometimes that's hard because we've been keeping ourselves under wraps for our entire lives.

Shame keeps us fake.

When I was a newlywed, we were struggling. Mostly we were struggling because my pregnancy hormones made me a little bit psycho. Many of these battles ended with me in a Wendy's drive-through ordering a lonely bacon cheeseburger because Graham fell asleep and wouldn't fight with me anymore.

If I had asked someone, I probably would have found out how normal this was. I probably would have discovered that I wasn't the only one to struggle in the first year of marriage. But I didn't.

I had shame and I just didn't talk about it. For months and months I didn't talk about it. I hung out with friends and talked about everything but "it."

One day, I don't know why exactly, I was sitting in a friend's living room and I just let it all spill. All my struggles, all my fears, and all my I-don't-know-how-to-do-this exasperations. I was like a liter of Coke that had been shaken up so much it finally exploded. My friends listened calmly and graciously, they asked questions, and then they said the thing my heart needed to hear: "I totally get it; I've been there."

Is there anything better than opening up and being met with gracious understanding? Is there anything better than being met with a "me too" or an "I've been there" or an "I'm here"? Is there anything better than getting all those pent-up feelings out on the table and being loved and accepted for who you are and where you are? Is there anything better than being truly known without secrets? Is there anything better than not being lonely in your struggle anymore?

I don't know if there is.

When you open up your heart, even the dark places, and are met with love and empathy, it's nothing short of a spiritual experience.

In friendship, we have a choice. We can keep things light and fluffy and easy. We can dip our toes in but keep our cards close. We can be vulnerable, but just a little. We can bury our struggles so there's no possibility of rejection. *Or* we can be true to ourselves. We can take the risk of showing up all the way in our friendships. We can dive into the deep and tell it like it is. We can share the things that are sacred and private, painful and true.

It's easy to stay in the safe zone because of the what-ifs. What if they reject us when they really know us? What if they judge us? What if they don't love us anymore?

Friend, can I say something to you? If your fear is realized, and at the first sign of vulnerability your friends drop you like you're hot, then sister, those are not your friends.

Those are not your friends, and that's not what friendship is.

Friendship should be a pressure-free zone.

Friendship should be the place where we can erupt like a volcano, laugh like a lunatic, and cry our ugliest without ever feeling judged. It should be a place for our unedited thoughts because we know we won't be judged even if we're wrong. It should be the place to be too much. It should be the place to be loud and obnoxious. It should be the place to be tired and empty. It should be the place to be quiet and just share space. We shouldn't have to force ourselves to talk louder or find something to say, and we shouldn't have to turn down the volume or edit ourselves either.

⟨⟨⟨⟨⟨⟨

I have always longed for sisterhood.

My deepest desire was to have friends that I could call my sisters. I wanted friends who would walk in my house and open the fridge. I wanted friends who knew me well enough to call me out when needed, friends who I didn't have to perform for. Friends who would be with me when things were hard. I wanted the familiarity, the belonging, the closeness, the knowing-what-she's-thinking-before-she-says-it kind of friendship. When I learned that I had the power to give that kind of friendship away, it changed everything. It turned out that when I gave away sisterhood, I also found it.

If you're longing for something more than fake, something more than superficial, something more than "I'm good, thanks, how are you?" then girl, start with you. You don't have to wait. Every time you're vulnerable and share a piece of your heart, it's an invitation to the listener—whether you know it or not. Your authenticity says, "I'm real, and I'm not scared of your real if you want to share it."

What Now?

Create Space. I don't mean a literal space like your house (although it can be that too); I mean a space that you bring with you wherever you go. A space you bring to the park for a play-date, and a space you bring to happy hour on Tuesday night. The space is comfortable, and it's inviting. It doesn't need to have fancy furniture from Restoration Hardware or dusted shelves. It doesn't need to have freshly vacuumed carpet lines or fancy snacks and bottled water. It doesn't need to have a PhD in friendship or know how to cartwheel. It can have those things if you want, but those aren't the most important things. The most important thing is that it's lived-in and warm. The most important part of all is that you give an invitation to come and sit awhile, to come and be as you are. It's a space that says, *Happy? Sad? Struggling? Perfect, I get it, and I won't judge you.* It's a space that says you belong.

Get Real. Vulnerability attracts vulnerability. If your conversations are stuck on elementary schools for your kids and what TV show you're watching, maybe it's time to take a risk and drop a truth bomb just to see what happens. It can be anything. It can be about how your anxiety has been flaring up and you're having a hard time sleeping at night. It can be about how you're worried if you're doing a good job raising your kids. It can be about how you're having a crisis of faith and you're struggling to hear God. It can be anything as long as it's real.

Invite. Now invite people in. Ask questions that are deeper than "Who does your hair?" Ask how their hearts are. Ask how they really are. Ask how they've been handling current events or how motherhood is going. If you know they're going through something hard, gently ask about it. If they're grieving, check in on them. If they're going through a divorce, ask about it.

Build Your Table. Build the table you've always longed to be invited to.

8

WHEN YOU'RE STUCK
ON THE OUTSIDE

love, Amy

When my husband and I moved to our town, I knew no one.
And I didn't know where anything was—not even the Target, and
yeah, that was hard because I really love Target.

I love the dollar section. I love the beauty section. I love the
Starbucks and the aroma right when you walk in, and oh my
word, I love their welcome mats and their throw pillows and the
office supplies. Don't even get me started. Sharpies fill my soul
with so much gladness. I do not, however, love the cameras in

the self-checkout line. Those things are brutal. If you've ever felt personally attacked by one, I would like to gently remind you that they are lying to you. You're a beautiful goddess, and no, your nose doesn't look that way and your skin isn't really gray and chalky.

When we first moved, I would have done anything for a friend—one single friend.

I had a beautiful, beautiful newborn, who had colic and cried relentlessly. I had an amazing husband who was and is my home, who worked often. I was racked with loneliness, but I was also determined not to stay that way. So I went out and I talked to people. It was weird.

I'd go to the grocery and look for any reason to connect with other women.

"Oh my word! I love prepackaged shredded cheese too! I can't believe this! What are the chances? Would you like to get coffee sometime since we obviously have so much in common?"

I'd go to the park and look for friends. That was dumb because I had a newborn, so he wasn't going down the slide or anything. He wasn't even sitting up on the grass and couldn't be pushed in the swing. I just held him, stood there aimlessly, and hoped someone would eventually talk to me. They usually didn't, but I was desperate. Sometimes I'd be an arm's length away from a group of women and would stand there and pray to be noticed.

Someone, anyone, please say hi to me. Tell me I have Dorito breath. I don't care. Just say something. I hadn't had an actual conversation with another human besides my husband in so long. I'd do my best to chat up cashiers, but the people pleaser in me would get all flustered and stressed out when someone walked up behind me in the line. I didn't want to make them mad, ya know? So I'd tell the cashiers to have a nice day and move along with my life.

I tried church, but church is hard when you're new. It's hard when you walk in and see the giant sanctuary and you have no idea where to sit, so you stay close to the back rows. It's hard when you're a new mom, and your baby starts crying, or worse, when they spit up all over the pew, and everything smells disgusting. It's hard when you've still got some extra baby weight hanging onto your hips and your stomach and none of your dresses fit and your boobs are massive, and it's hard when you see everyone gathered up in little huddles and you don't see an open space for you to make your way in anywhere.

The closest family we had was five hours away, and when we'd go back to visit, I'd laugh and tell them I was about to start standing on the side of the street with a sign that said, "Please just be my friend. I'm not a psycho, and I'll tell you you're pretty, and I'll let you pick the restaurant." Maybe I'd even learn to flip the sign and do all of that business like the people who dress up as the Statue of Liberty outside of insurance companies. If I didn't think it would have eventually ended with me on *Dateline*, I probably would have done this for real.

You know what the craziest part of it is? I would have made a fantastic friend at the time. I wouldn't have forgotten to text back. I wouldn't have been distracted. I wouldn't have had a hard time finding a date where our schedules worked out because I had absolutely nothing going on outside of my home. Inside of my home, sure, I was doing the job of ten people, but I didn't have a lot on my calendar. I did, however, have a lot of time, energy, and love to give.

During this hard season, I learned all about loneliness, and I learned all about heartbreak, and I learned all about not having my name on the invite list. I learned all about life on the outside of the circle, and to this day, I will tell you it is one of the greatest things I've ever learned because it taught me to appreciate every single piece of who I am (except maybe my voice—I dunno why, but I'm working on that one).

Becoming isn't an easy thing.

Growing doesn't come without some pain.

Learning doesn't come without some tough lessons.

Before God gives you the microphone, he's going to make you walk the mountain. Before you find success, he's going to let you struggle. Before you get the gold, he's going to let you dig your way through a good bit of garbage.

I love helping women who ache with loneliness because I've been lonely. I've walked in their shoes. I've tasted their tears. We might have sat in different closets and wondered what in the world is wrong with us in different ways, but we survived the same storms, and there is something beautiful about those sacred shared experiences. They bring us together. They bring out our ability to empathize, and they often bring out our deepest passions. The places where we have been the most hurt are usually the places that make us want to be the most helpful to others.

〳〵〲〳〵

Being strange to strangers at the grocery store absolutely did not work in my favor. I'm lucky I didn't end up with a restraining order or something. Nobody wanted to bond over mozzarella.

"Will the woman in aisle 5 wearing a messy bun and a graphic tee please stop harassing fellow customers? They do not want to talk to you, and you're sketching everyone out. Also, M&M's are buy one get one half off. Thank you for shopping."

And the phrase "find your people" is especially unhelpful when you're in the midst of loneliness. Every time I read a book or scrolled across a Facebook post telling me to find my people, I wanted to puke and possibly punch some things.

I get it. Having people is awesome. But hooooow? For the love, stop rubbing your happy friendships in my face, please, and just tell me where to look for these so-called people because they seem to be hiding.

So how did I do it?

First, I put myself out there, and I focused on finding common ground with the people I did meet. Now, the common ground probably needs to be something deeper than a food item every single person in America consumes on a regular basis, but it doesn't need to be anything especially fancy either. I met a girl named Reagan between the shoe department and the perfume counter at the mall. We had babies about the same age, and as we got to talking, we realized that I had worked with her sister a few years prior. I'll never know why, and I'll never forget her kindness, but Reagan invited my husband and me to have pizza that night with a few friends. That is how I met my first friend in my town, Reagan. That is how I met my second friend in my town, Rachel. And through Rachel, I can't even count how many others I met. We're still friends to this day—almost nine years later—and I'm grateful every single day.

I put myself out there, and even though I swung a few times and missed, I finally knocked it out of the park with Reagan. That friendship became a segue for almost every other friend I would go on to make. One person can make a huge difference. One conversation can change everything. One connection can make a new town feel like home. Don't ever forget that, and don't ever give up. The next person could be the right person.

Second, I finally asked my friends if they knew any women in town they could introduce me to. I put the word out on Facebook, and I was terrified to do it. I was so scared people would think I was desperate, but the truth is that I was. I *was* desperate, and I'd rather be desperate than lonely any day of the week. That post didn't get a lot of likes, and it didn't get a lot of comments, but my friend Ashley totally delivered. She had a friend named Lindsey who lived near me, and she introduced us through a group text message. Lindsey happened to have a baby close to the age of mine, and we became fast friends. Soon we were dropping off Diet Cokes and stopping by each other's houses just to hang out and help each other fold laundry. I was there when she got divorced. I was there when she got remarried. I was there when she gave birth to her third baby—like seriously, she started pushing almost before I could run out of the room yelling "I love you" and singing Salt-N-Pepa lyrics before closing the door behind me. Let's just say, I've seen a lot of Lindsey. Lindsey eventually moved a few hours away, and while long-distance friendships don't lend themselves to showing up in pajamas and raggedy T-shirts, they're still pretty special.

And finally, I found the outsider, like myself. Her name was Callie. I'd been living in this town for a few years at that point, and I had worked and worked to force my way in with a particular group. I'd extended invitations. I'd reached out. I'd initiated conversations. I thought I was part of the group. And then I found out there was a girls' night and I hadn't been included. That's when something clicked: I thought of these women as my friends, but they did not feel the same way about me. I was simply some nice girl they kinda knew, and I realized I'd been going about pursuing friendship all wrong. I was trying to beg my way into a group that didn't have an open spot.

I remained cordial and friendly, of course. I didn't stop liking them. It wasn't their fault they felt more of a connection with one another. But good people don't always make good friends, so I stopped trying so hard. And then I remembered: the people who make the best friends are usually the ones who need a best friend, so I started thinking about everyone else who might have been an outsider too, and Callie came to mind. She was new in town, and I knew exactly how that felt.

And now, years later, Callie has become more like a sister to me than anything else. If I'm going to the store, without hesitation, I grab her favorite bag of pretzels. She picks my kids up from school and brings them to her house to play at least once a week. I keep her kids' favorite snacks stocked in my refrigerator, and they feel comfortable enough at my house to go digging for food without even asking. I love that. We have matching french fry and hamburger sweatshirts, and neither of us cares how cheesy that is. I know her parents. I have her Starbucks order memorized. I go over and feed her cats when she's out of town. I even clean their litter box, which is so disgusting, but I do it with a smile, because it's for Callie. (I still think she needs a dog, but that's neither here nor there.) We hang out on Friday nights eating pizza and playing card games just because. We very much do life together, and it has been, without a doubt, one of the most meaningful friendships of my adult life. She has set the bar high for what a friend should be.

Instead of forcing my way into the middle of a closed circle, the answer to my prayers was waiting on the outside all along. I just had to open my eyes, recognize it, and then be brave enough to initiate.

When you create your own space, remember what it's like to wonder if anybody really wants you there. Remember what it's like not to know anyone. Remember what it's like to stand there like an awkward turtle, twiddling your thumbs, talking to yourself, counting down the minutes until you can get the heck out and curl up on your couch with your first love, Netflix. Remember what it's like to not be included in a conversation and to have to pretend to scroll your phone just so you have something to do. Remember how it hurts not to belong in the circle, and leave some space for new sisters to be instantly included.

Circles can be awfully cruel. They can be cliquish and childish. They can be excluding and oh-my-gosh exhausting. Build your own space and look around and gather up all the women you notice hanging outside of that tight radius. You will find some of your best friends there. That's where you are going to find people who are every bit as hungry for connection as you are. And while it's important to find people who get your jokes, I'm telling you that maybe the most important ingredient in friendship is finding friends who crave it the same way you do—friends who will prioritize it and cherish it. Friends who have room for it and room for you.

In a perfect world, we'd have the capacity, the energy, and the time to be best friends with everyone. We'd be incredibly close and bonded with every person we liked. We would share our secrets with them. We would communicate with them regularly, and we would feel safe with them. But we don't live in that world. We live in a world where humans have limitations. Even you. You're crazy awesome, but you have to sleep sometimes and stuff. You only have twenty-four hours in a day, seven days in a week, and you have obligations. No matter how hard you try, how wonderful your intentions may be, or how much effort you put into it, you can't be best friends with everyone, and that doesn't make you a bad person. It simply makes you a person.

Now, hang on with me here because I'm about to get very technical and researchie. Try not to be intimidated by how incredibly smart and sophisticated the next few paragraphs are going to make me sound.

While studying the grooming habits of nonhuman primates, British anthropologist Robin Dunbar discovered there was a correlation between brain size and the size of one's social circle. Dunbar realized what a valuable tool this would be if he could apply this principle to humans, and what he found was that groups consistently fell into the range of about 150 members. Any more than that, and the group was unlikely to last long. This became known as Dunbar's number.[1]

Now, 150 isn't the only important number in his findings. These numbers exist almost in layers. Fifteen hundred, on the very outskirts, is the number of people we are capable of recognizing. One layer in, 500 is the number of people we are able to hold as acquaintances. Because of social media, we are inundated with these two layers, but these layers do almost nothing to satisfy our desire for connection. We recognize a lot of people. We know who a lot of people are, but that's not what we want. We don't want to know who someone is, we want to know someone deeply and personally, and we want them to know us in return.

One more layer inward, we find the 150 meaningful contacts. These are the people you would invite to a really large party—a wedding perhaps. This is likely the number of people on our Christmas card lists (or in my case, Valentine's card list because I can never get it together in the month of December).

Once that layer is peeled, we find we are capable of maintaining about fifty loose friendships. (If this number makes you want to cry a little because you don't feel like you have fifty loose friendships, it's okay. It made me gasp too.)

Another layer in, Dunbar found humans typically limit themselves to fifteen good friends. These are the people we would invite to a birthday celebration or a more intimate dinner party. These are the people we keep up with regularly. We would truly miss them if they were no longer in our lives. We celebrate their presence, and we mourn their absence.

Now we come to the layer that fascinates us the most. This is the tightest group. These are our people. These are our beloveds. These are the ones we trust with our most intimate secrets, the ones who feel like home and let us know we belong. At the very core, we have enough room for about five "best friends." These people have the most significance in our lives. They make our worlds brighter and better. They impact who we are, what we believe, and how we live in very real ways.

Keep in mind, these numbers are all relative. There are several factors that come into play. For instance, gender and age both play a role. Personality also matters. More extroverted people tend to have larger networks, while introverts put their energy into less-concentrated pools.

Consider a ruler. The number on a standard ruler will always be twelve inches. It doesn't matter where you hold it, who holds it, or which direction it goes in; the number will always stay the same. If you hold it horizontally, you will see the number twelve, but things will stay shallow. The number is the same, but there is no depth. But if you hold the ruler vertically, things flip. Again, the number is the same, but now there's depth.

This is how it is with our friends.

If we spread ourselves thin, our social circles are likely going to be robust. This is popularity at its finest. Whereas if we put the majority of our focus on just a few folks, we might not be considered the coolest kids in town. We might not throw huge parties, and we might not be invited to book clubs or wine nights. Our phones might not ring off the hook, and we may not be included in a ton of group texts. But we can be the kind of women who hold someone's struggles and carry someone's burdens. We can be the kind of women who hold space for our closest circle of confidants.

There's no real right or wrong here. We all value friendship differently, and we all prioritize it in different ways. There is no universal number. What works for you may not work for the person sitting next to you, and what worked for you in high school probably doesn't work for you in your thirties. Things change. People change, and that's okay. But when choosing who to invest in, there are some universal principles.

Invest in people who are like-hearted. Invest in people who are capable of investing in you. Invest in people who make room for you at their tables. Invest in people who are dependable. Invest in people who are consistent and willing to get real. Invest in people who make you feel a sense of connection, and even more importantly, a sense of belonging.

I don't know where you'll find your people, but I know I found mine because I finally stopped trying to beg, force, and claw my way into the center of a circle, and I started looking on the outside.

If you don't have a place to belong, it's essential that you don't dwell in that hurt. Instead, dedicate yourself to the process of building something better. Cry your tears. Feel your feelings. They are real, and it is painful. You can visit, but that hurt absolutely cannot be where you decide to set up tent. There are so many lonely women who depend on your bravery, and if you build it, maybe they'll come. And maybe they won't. We have to accept that we have zero control over other people's actions. Zero. Nada. Zip. Zilch. It is possibly the hardest lesson in life, but I genuinely believe it is one of the first steps to climbing the ladder toward happiness.

Do it for them. Do it for other women. Do it out of necessity. Do it out of love. But know there is a very, very good chance that as you build a home for others to come alive, you'll find a place of belonging for yourself as well.

I know being left out hurts, but I also know that hard times don't have to harden you. If you'll let them, they can be the things that strengthen your spirit and soften your heart. They can be the things that mold you and shape you into the exact woman you were always born to become. God has a funny way of taking our very deepest cuts and allowing us to use them to help others heal.

Don't focus on the invitations you didn't get. Don't focus on the group texts you were left off of or the birthday parties where you weren't included. Don't focus on all of those things you can't control. Focus on you.

Focus on how you reach out to others.

Focus on how you give.

Focus on how you become salt and light and all the beautiful things. Who knows? You may just be the answer to someone else's lonely prayer.

I didn't know it back then, but being left out was the best thing that ever happened to me. I'm grateful for it every single day, and I pray you learn to appreciate it as well. When you've healed, the story reads much differently than it did when you were bleeding everywhere.

Don't let your experiences go to waste. Please. I am begging you.

Use them.

Use them to recognize the hurting among you. Use them to recognize the lonely. Use them to recognize the left out. And then use them to reach out a hand.

The world needs those experiences. The world needs those stories. The world needs you.

What Now?

Deep breaths. I know it's painful, and I know you're feeling the sting of rejection, but look for ways that beauty and redemption can come from your brokenness. Look around you. Be aware. You'll probably realize you aren't the only one who's on the outside. Be bold enough to gather those women on the outskirts and start something new. This is your life. You don't have to wait for an invitation to the party; you can throw your own, and you can even pick the theme and the appetizers. (Pigs in a blanket are the best, though.)

Find someone who needs a friend and get to know her. Make a list of women who may also be needing friendship and reach out to them. Think about women at your church, other moms at your kids' school, the women who always sit in the back during yoga. Ask them to lunch. Find them at the next event and initiate a conversation. Pull back when you are spreading yourself too thin. Look up hobby groups in your town and get involved. Find a Mothers of Preschoolers (MOPS) group or a Bible study. Be consistent in showing up with confidence.

9

WHEN YOU CRAM ALL YOUR JUNK IN THE CLOSET AND SLAM THE DOOR

love, Jess

My mother-in-law is the best hostess. She makes everyone feel at home. When you walk into her kitchen it smells like home-made bread, and there's always a candle burning. She's stirring and adding spices and pulling things out of the fridge like she's feeding an army. She'll hand you a cutting board and veggies to chop at the table as she asks you about your day, your plans for the future, and why you haven't put snow tires on your car yet. She makes you feel like the most interesting person in the entire world. She makes you feel so fascinating that once someone thought she was a spy. That was an unfortunate turn of events. The rest of us embrace it, though, because who else in the entire world is going to care what we ate for lunch today? It's nice to be that interesting sometimes.

For a long time, I couldn't understand why my husband would come home from work and give me an entire play-by-play of his day. "Well, I drove up US 2 this morning and then took the shortcut over to Willow Glen. Saw a few deer on the way, didn't hit any. I stopped by the gas station and grabbed a few gallons and coffee before heading to the job . . ."

It was as though I were receiving a book report of the most mundane aspects of his life. Finally, I asked him why he told me all this information with the exuberance of a corpse, and he said, "Oh, well if my mom asked me about my day and I didn't do that, she'd ask me a million questions afterward."

We are so lucky to be loved by her.

From the first moment I sat at her table, I wanted to have my own table like hers. She doesn't just feed people—she creates space for them to belong. It is a gift. Once I asked her to share one of her hosting secrets. "Well," she said, "I used to always shove all my piles of paper that I had around the kitchen in my stove when company came over."

My father-in-law snorted knowingly at this statement. "Yes, she did."

"You know, bills and important things like that."

"Important things," added my father-in-law, raising one eyebrow at me like he couldn't wait for the punch line.

"Until one night I forgot and I accidentally lit it all on fire."

They both roared with laughter. "So now I hide it other places." She smirked.

I learned from the best.

※※

In modern society we're not just dealing with the normal (age-old) insecurity about our flaws, we're also dealing with the pressure of social media. Our feeds are full of curated homes and toned physiques. Subconsciously it's easy to buy into the lie that we have to be impressive in order to be loved, but listen to me because this is important: the number of times that little heart button is pushed has absolutely nothing to do with love. Nothing. At. All. Being admired is a whole lot different from being loved. From what I can tell, real love can only grow in vulnerability and authenticity.

When you approach friendship, you have to turn off that part of your brain that wants to put a filter over your life to make the wrinkles go away. Maybe you don't want your wrinkles on Instagram, but bring your wrinkles and under eye circles and cellulite to your friendships because that's where they belong.

Invite people into your life as is. Your face as is, your heart as is, your thighs as is.

I learned the formal way to set a table when I was a Daisy Girl Scout, but now that I'm an adult, I've discovered that paper plates are more how I roll.

I'm a hostess who hides her mess in the coat closet and slams the door before it all avalanches its way onto the floor. I'm the hostess who never has enough forks. It's cool if I eat with my hands bear-style, right? I'm the hostess who, one time, forgot the correct ingredients for boxed brownies and nearly made my guest lose a crown on her back tooth. (It was so nice of you to try them; just send me the bill for the dentist, Brenda. Here's some wine to wash that down. I hope you're not constipated later.)

It's normal to feel like you have to hide. It's natural to hide away. It's normal to feel like your house isn't nice enough to host and what you have isn't enough to measure up. But good things are rarely easy, and easy things are rarely good. Friendship works best with vulnerability, open arms, and an open-door policy. In fact, friendship only works when vulnerability is welcomed.

When you walk into my mother-in-law's kitchen the very first time, you won't get offered a cutting board or a broom to help get things ready. You'll be ushered into the living room to have a glass of wine by the fire while she finishes things up. But once you've been there a few times, you just might receive that honor. It sounds funny, but it's the truth—it is an honor. Sitting in her warm kitchen peeling potatoes makes you feel like you're a part of the story. You see the mess, the hustle, the pot of noodles boiling over on the stove, and the timer telling you the cookies are done. It's an honor to be a part of someone else's life, and mess is an important, irreplaceable part of that.

It's those evenings—the evenings setting the table and rushing to check the bread because something is burning—that make me feel like I am really part of the family. Those are the evenings that make me want a table just like hers.

The first time I have someone over, I sweep underneath my chairs and make my bed. Once we get to know each other, I'll ask if we could keep things casual tonight because I just want to wear my pajamas. Pajama nights are the best. Nothing makes me happier than when my friends show up in their sweats and messy buns and faces that say today was a *day*.

Your mess doesn't make you unfriendable; it's actually the opposite. If you invite people into your mess, you're creating space for them to have their mess too. I know exactly zero people who don't have some mess. Maybe it's not house mess; maybe their mess is a broken relationship, maybe it's a broken heart. Maybe their mess is anxiety or depression. Maybe it's financial struggle, maybe it's health. Maybe their mess is past pain or the constant feeling of not being enough. We all have messes.

There are only two ways to deal with mess. We can embrace it and be real about it, or we can be ashamed of it and hide it. The first one can lead to fulfilling friendships, the second one leads to a whole lot of loneliness. Letting people into our messes is one of the scariest things we can do, but it offers redemption that the alternative does not. In fact, it seems to me that the only way shame is totally broken is in the context of relationship. I think God must have made it that way on purpose because he didn't want us doing life alone.

It's true that some people aren't going to be worthy of your vulnerability. Some people will turn up their noses at your perceived flaws. They'll see your humanity as failure. They'll judge you for how clean (or not clean) your house is. They'll judge you for your personality, for the things you say, and for the way you do life. Let me tell you something (and I can't stress this enough): those are not your people. Bless them and let them go. Life is too short to spend it trying to impress people who didn't like you in the first place. The truth is, if they're not comfortable with your humanity, they're probably not comfortable with theirs either, and that's not yours to deal with. In my mind, friendship is walking through life together. It's walking through the muddy pits (and falling face first) and dancing through the grassy meadows and laughing, crying, and belonging the whole way through. Any other kind of friendship just doesn't seem worth the time.

I've had a few friends in my life who thought I needed "fixing." Not an "I love you, and also you have salad in your teeth" kind of fixing; more like a "you'd be better if you were different" kind of fixing. I'm not going to lie—it hurt. At times it took me a while to realize what was going on, but once I caught on, I determined that if someone didn't like me, I clearly wasn't the friend for them (and they weren't for me). I want to be humble and grow when there are things in my life that need adjusting, but there's a big difference between growing and changing who you are altogether. If who I am rubs someone wrong, then that's not my person.

A few years ago I had a friend who, it turned out, didn't really like me. I don't think she actively hated me, I just think she never fully embraced me for me. The first sign was a string of what felt like constant confrontations. She felt I'd let so-and-so down, or she thought I could do this a little differently. I thought it was strange that she was so quick to accuse me, but I sloughed off any weirdness and chalked it up to misunderstandings and different personalities. A little while later she got heated with me about something else. Again I let it go. *Whatever, we're all different, and I definitely am not perfect.* A week later she had another issue with me. It kept happening and happening. What I did was wrong, what I said was wrong, how I handled that was wrong. Finally I had my aha moment. I realized she was bothered by the essence of who I was. I rubbed her the wrong way. I don't think she would have admitted that, but her actions spoke the truth. She was quick to accuse me because she'd never really embraced me in the first place.

Beware of people who try to turn you into a reflection of themselves. That's not where you belong, sister. I was super-duper different from this nonfriend, and that's probably why I grated against her. But it doesn't always have to be that way. I have friends who are as different from me as pickles are to jalapeños, but we've learned to embrace our differences and are better for it.

I adore my friend Erika. She is order; I am chaos. She drinks organic tea and hasn't been to a fast-food restaurant in years. I drink quad espressos and count spicy chicken sandwiches from Chick-fil-A on my list of favorite things. When we get together, I'm often still sweaty from my morning run and pounding a coffee. She's dressed, clean, and smells like she just walked out of Anthropologie. She is intentional and cautious; I am random and a risk-taker. She thinks before she talks; I talk before I think. Her favorite day would be spent at the spa; mine would probably be spent at the amusement park. I'm bad about interrupting when I'm excited. She's bad at being on time. We're so different, but we're better together.

I have a friend who loves using her tractor and growing vege-tables. She's also a phenomenal homeschool teacher, but when she describes how much fun she's having crafting the alphabet out of fresh bread dough, I tell her that everything she's saying is giving me a panic attack. I have a friend who loves old movies and being a homebody (I can be a homebody for approximately two hours at a time before I start to implode). I have friends who are observant and detailed (I wouldn't notice a grizzly unless it bit off my arm). I have friends who are driven and natural achievers (when given the choice between accomplishing something and having fun, I will always choose fun).

I am so different from each of these friends, but it works. You know why? Because we love each other for who we are. We love each other with our mess. We've learned to laugh when we drive each other crazy, and we don't ever try to change the other person. Connection comes when we stop measuring ourselves against one another and embrace the idea that we are all beautifully imperfect. I'm never going to be like them, and they're never going to be like me, but we are better together. I love who they are, and I'm grateful for what their strengths bring to my life.

Here's the truth: I'm not going to start hiding myself in order to be palatable to someone who doesn't deserve me. I'm going to find people who show me they're worthy of the real me so that I can invite them to be a deeper part of my life.

We cannot belong if we don't share our truths. We cannot belong unless we let the ones who have earned it see our closets shoved full of crap. I'm not saying you need to give them a tour immediately (*Hey, welcome to my home. Would you like to see my garage? It's like a thrift store got burglarized out there!*), but I am saying that showing others your unfiltered life is one of the crucial steps to close friendship.

‹‹‹‹‹

Several years ago I stopped being okay. I'm not sure if it happened suddenly or if it was a process so slow I didn't see the change until it was too late. I just woke up one morning with what felt like a ton of bricks sitting on my chest. My usual happy-go-lucky self was completely gone, just vanished.

It reminded me of when I was twelve and got such bad poison oak on my face that when I looked in the mirror I cried because I couldn't recognize myself behind the swollen eyes and cheeks. My anxiety terrified me because I didn't know this person wandering around my house like a zombie unable to function or be a mom to my kids.

I'd experienced anxiety before, but this was debilitating anxiety. I was usually always on the go, bringing my kids to the beach or to the park, but I couldn't leave my house at all without sobbing and shaking with no control or ability to stop.

It was all I could do to text my friends. My friend Aubree had been in the trenches with anxiety for years and had always invited me into that mess. She knew what to do. She showed up at my house the next day. We sat on the porch. My body was hunched over and defeated. My face was pale, and my skin couldn't seem to soak up the sun that was all around us. "What are you afraid of today?" she asked me.

And with that, I let it out. I was terrified to tell her, as though giving voice to the awful fears would make them come true, but I did it anyway. She listened quietly until I was done, and then she looked into my eyes. "Not going to happen," she said with absolute assurance. "All that is just anxiety." She waited for me to soak that in. "I promise you that there's no truth in those fears."

And then I wept. I ugly cried there on the porch with her and found relief for the first time since I'd woken up that morning.

She did that every day for a month until my anxiety spell finally broke.

She let me into her mess first, and she made it easy for me to let her into mine. She let me see the hard parts of her life and not just the happy parts she posted on Instagram.

Letting people into our struggles isn't an optional part of friendship.

Vulnerability is the key to closeness. I don't know how I would have navigated that without her. When I look back on that time in my life, I don't feel pain; I feel something else. I feel grateful because she stood with me in the hard place, and now that will always be a part of our story, an unbreakable part of our story.

My "mess" that I shove in the closet might be completely different from yours. Maybe you're not messy at all. Maybe you're superclean and orderly, and your "mess" is that you're struggling in your marriage. All of our messes are different, but we're all deserving of belonging.

Connection comes when we see a friend's true self and we don't judge her or ourselves because neither of us deserves it.

I love Aubs, she loves me, and together we're better.

〰

I have two levels of vulnerability. The first is just me living my life authentically. Brand-new friends (and even sometimes strangers) get to see that level, and if they don't like it, oh well, it's not going to bother me that much. That level includes my car doubling as my closet and being chock-full of shoes, coats, socks, and random wrappers (thanks, kids). It includes me running to the store pre-coffee with my face still puffy and the dark circles under my eyes being enhanced by a smudge of mascara. I do not look good, and that's okay. It includes stories from my past that no longer cause me shame. It includes (sometimes oversharing) my own mistakes and mishaps because I like to make people laugh and feel more comfortable in their own skin.

The second level is my real, my deep, and my sacred. I treat that level of vulnerability like a diamond, and I'm careful who I give it away to. That level is the one where I pull out all the stops. It includes ugly crying and my deepest struggles. It includes things I'm still walking out and haven't come all the way through yet. It includes talking about wounds that haven't yet healed and things that do cause me a pang of shame. It includes talking about my insecurities. It includes opening up about my marriage and my kids.

Your list might be different from mine. Maybe you're not comfortable with puffy eyes and smudged mascara until level two—that's okay. Maybe you're comfortable talking about your current struggles in level one—that's also okay. What I'm saying is, you don't have to give your diamonds away to everyone. It's important to give them away to the people who are worthy and to those who have earned your trust. A certain level of vulnerability is key to growing friendship at any level, but it's absolutely okay—and necessary—to pace yourself.

Do not wait until you have yourself together. Do not wait until you have a bigger house to host in or your life is absent of struggle. Invite people into your life now. Be like my mother-in-law. Throw open your door and offer a chair at the table. When you're ready, hand them a potato to peel and ask them about their life.

Six years ago we sold our house and lived in a camper for the summer. We put our kitchen table under a tree and strung some lights. We didn't have a "home," but we invited our friends over, and they came anyway. We spent long nights sitting in camp chairs around the fire, and we made memories we all still cherish.

Life is full and messy. It's never going to be perfect, and you're never going to be all together, and I think that's the point. Friendship is not a stage on which you have to perform, and it isn't a popularity contest. True friendship is where messes belong.

Invite people into your life *as is*. Don't wait for things to slow down. Don't wait to stop struggling with depression. Don't wait till you have a big enough dining room table. Don't wait to fit into those pants. Don't wait until you know how to cook something other than roast. Don't wait, and don't be scared to let them see your mess.

Every time you invite someone into your mess, you create space for them to invite you into theirs too.

What Now?

It's scary to let people see our messes. Social media makes us feel even more isolated and unable to share our struggles because we're comparing ourselves to a feed full of good lighting and great hair.

The best way to rip off the Band-Aid is to just do it. What is one way you can get more vulnerable and real with your friends this week? Maybe it's inviting someone over and not worrying about the sink full of dishes and the laundry on the couch. Maybe it's getting more real and raw in your conversations with a friend. Maybe it's not cleaning up your living room floor before you take that pic to post. Maybe it's answering someone honestly when they ask you "how are you?" Maybe it's throwing out those jeans that threaten to cut off your circulation or damage an organ every time you manage to button them. Maybe it's just telling the truth in whatever way it's comfortable for you to tell it.

Sometimes if I'm having a bad day and I'm not sure how to "not pretend" around my friends, I'll send a text ahead of time that says something like "I'm in a really bad mood today, I didn't sleep well, and I'm on my period, so if I act weird, that's why" or "Hey, I fought with Graham this morning, so I'm in a bit of a funk, just wanted you to know." Somehow that simple action empowers me to just be.

Sister, friendship is exactly where your mess belongs.

10

WHEN IT ALL FEELS LIKE
HIGH SCHOOL 2.0

love, Amy

I'll never forget casually scrolling on Instagram one morn-ing (dooot de doot da doo) while standing in front of my bathroom mirror putting on blush and foundation and all of that and noticing a picture of my closest friends together out of the corner of my eye.

This couldn't be right. Maybe I'd seen wrong.

So I clicked backward.

Nope. There it was. Plain as day for everyone to see.

And the caption hit even harder: "Love when my girls all get together!"

Ouch. Up until thirty seconds ago, I'd thought I was one of the girls. *I guess not.*

Punch straight to the gut. And a little to the heart too.

Wait, did I miss a text? Did I overlook something? Had we all planned this together a week ago, and I'd completely forgotten? I could be like that sometimes. Or maybe it was an old picture. *Duh. That would make sense.*

I scrolled back through my messages, thinking there must be a simple explanation, something I'd missed.

Nope. Nothing there.

I didn't give up hope. I genuinely felt like there was a perfectly logical reason I didn't get an invite, and I thought we were close enough that I could bring up the subject without it getting weird. I loved these girls. I believed with my whole, entire being that we were "in it." They would never do this to me.

I just knew everything would be fine.

I normally go straight to panic mode in situations like these—anything where there is the slightest chance of conflict ensuing—and I tend to assume the worst, but this time I really didn't. I trusted these friends too much not to give them the benefit of the doubt.

So, I picked up my phone and made the call.

"Hey girl, um . . . I am sure this isn't a big deal, but I'm over here kind of stressing and kind of hurt, but before I jump to conclusions, I just thought I'd call. Um . . . did y'all go out last night and not invite me? It's really no big deal. I just want to make sure I didn't do anything wrong."

I clearly caught her a little off guard. I got a very awkward, very scattered answer that made my chest sink. She simply passed the blame on to someone else, and I knew then and there, I was never going to get my answer.

It hadn't been a mistake after all.

I'd been intentionally left out, and I was deeply wounded.

Not only had I been left out of that one girls' night, but I'd been left out of group texts and stuff for a while, and I hadn't had a clue. I was hurt, sure, but more than that I was embarrassed.

I felt like a complete idiot.

In my mind, everyone in town was talking about me and gossiping about how I was just blowing my way through all these friend groups, making mistake after mistake, playing the part of the fool. (Note: They weren't. Nobody cared or thought anything about it except for me. I was stuck, but they were just out there living their lives—going to workout classes, picking up kids, making dinners, etc.)

How could I not have seen the signs?

I really thought things were reciprocal, and I really thought these were the friendships that were going to last a lifetime. I really thought things were different this go-round. I really cared about them. I really, really did and still do. To this day, they are some of my very favorite people, which is probably why their rejection cut so deep.

But in the snap of a finger, it felt like high school all over again. And I didn't particularly care for that stage of my life to say the least—besides the part where I could eat anything I wanted and still be a size 4. I liked that part, but the rest of it, blah.

I couldn't believe it.

There I was: unwanted, unliked, unincluded. I was sixteen years old—heartbroken, confused, terribly insecure, and all alone—all over again. I was the girl, standing there with her tray, who didn't know where to sit in the cafeteria.

Maybe I didn't belong anywhere.

Now, let me interject here and tell you that looking back, I wasn't completely innocent. I had tried to be a good friend. Scratch that. I'd tried to be a great friend. There isn't anything I wouldn't have done for those friends. If they had needed me at three in the morning, without hesitation, I would have rushed to their sides.

But had I been perfect? No, not even close.

I'd been overly focused on work and writing, and even when I was with them, I was somewhat disconnected. My brain was always running and trying to figure out what I needed to do next, and I wasn't appreciating the moment. I should have put work away, enjoyed their presence, and been there with them fully. Distractions got the best of me and made me a lousy friend. (Bonus tip: put your phone away when you're spending time with people. I leave mine in the car 99 percent of the time now because I don't want a stupid screen to lure me away from the loved ones sitting there in the flesh right in front of me.)

I see that now, and I am a different kind of friend today because of the things that happened then. Lessons learned in the most heartbreaking way, I suppose.

When a once-sweet relationship reaches a place where it's gone sour, rarely is there only one party at fault, and to refuse to accept our part of the blame or pick up our own pieces only prevents us from being able to complete the puzzle the next time around. If you want to move forward, acknowledge the places where you got it wrong. If you want to do better, own your stuff and take the next step.

Sometimes, I think we're afraid it's going to be too painful to address our failures, so we ignore them completely. But do you know what really hurts? Making the same mistake over and over again. Never growing, never changing, never learning. Standing completely steadfast in our stubborn, selfish ways.

I don't want to stay stuck in the past, but I do want to learn from it.

Every time something happens, this is the frame of mind I revert back to: *You don't have a place. You don't fit in here. You don't fit in there. That table is already full. That table can't stand you. You already tried that table once. You should probably just go hide in the bathroom.*

But I'm not the same girl I was back in high school. Not by a long shot, and I'm not confined by the same four walls I was then. I'm also not bound by the same expectations.

There is no homeroom. There is no tardy bell. And there are no core subjects I have to study for. (Thank goodness, because algebra was a beast. Amen? I'll take the liberty of answering for you here. *Yes, girl. Amen.*)

There is no one table I have to force myself to fit in with. There is no homecoming crown I have to compete for. There is no "Most Likely to Succeed" I have to measure up to. I'm not trying to make the A-team, the varsity squad, or make sure my face gets in the yearbook more than anyone else's. And nobody— nobody—is handing out any kind of superlatives.

We don't have to live like that anymore. Hallelujah. We can, and we absolutely should, live in freedom. God's not handing out cool points, and he definitely hasn't pitted us against one another. He doesn't do that to his creations. He doesn't compare his children. He isn't getting out his red pen and scribbling down an F the moment you get rejected.

We should be fighting for one another, but we can probably tone it down a notch when it comes to fighting with one another.

You can build any kind of table you want. You can sit in whatever chair is the most comfortable for you. Heck, you can sit on the floor or in a bean bag chair if you want. Sit on a stool or a bouncy ball, or lie down on a yoga mat. You can invite anyone and everyone.

Life isn't about being popular. It was never about being popular—we just didn't get it back then, but I hope we get it now. Truly, your worth does not come from the size of your circle or the number of texts you get in a day. You are not more valuable based on the number of voice mails sitting in your inbox or the number of compliments you get on your outfit. It doesn't matter whether you are out doing something every single weekend or you spend most Saturdays pushing back your cuticles and playing solitaire.

In high school, there's such a high priority on getting ahead of everyone else. So much of girls' time is spent obsessed with being the girl who has the most—the most friends, the most boyfriends, the most awards, the most As, the most extracurricular activities, the most clothes, the most parties to attend, but all that does is lead to competition, comparison, jealousy, self-doubt, impersonating, posing, pretending, pushing people down to get ahead, aaaaand (drumroll please) drama. *So much stinking drama.*

We have allowed too much of this immature mentality to spill over into our adult lives and into our adult friendships. It doesn't work. It doesn't fuel us, and at the end of the day, it doesn't feel very good either. It doesn't fill us. It doesn't serve us. It doesn't serve others, and it sure doesn't serve Jesus.

He didn't love others so that he could get ahead. He didn't live so that he could beat out everyone else. He didn't surround himself with his disciples so that he could look "cool."

He surrounded himself with them so that he could pour into their lives, so that all the goodness he held could spill into them, and so that everyone could rise higher. He surrounded himself with them so they could learn together and pray together and go out into the world hand in hand and make meaning from the madness; so they could encourage one another when things got tough and remind one another of the call that had been placed on their lives.

When we get our minds right, and we get into a secure, mature rhythm, the people around us rise right along with us—and that is the goal. That's the whole point of it all, the entire meaning of friendship: that we do it in a way that lifts everyone in the group. That we leave better off than we came and we are capable of showing more grace, more compassion, more love in the end than we did in the beginning. That we shine a little brighter out there in the world because of the people right here in our circle.

That we move from a "her vs. me" and dive headfirst into a place of "we."

We belong to a God of abundance, and so we have to believe that there is an ample supply of opportunities. He didn't make any of us by accident, and he didn't make any of us without a plan in mind. Nobody can take that plan away. Nobody can erase the call God has put on our lives. He did not lack creativity when he created the world, and so I have a hard time believing there is a limit on the amount of creativity he put in our hearts.

It's time we stop trying to steal each other's crowns. It's time we stop clawing at each other and climbing over each other to get ahold of something that was never meant for us. Her crown isn't going to fit you. It's not going to look good on you. Let her have it, and relax—what's meant for you will be for you.

When she gets ahead, it doesn't have to push you back, and when she wins, it doesn't mean you lose. When she comes in first, it doesn't mean you come in last, and when she crosses the finish line, it doesn't mean you don't get a medal. Turns out, none of us are even running the same race.

*

A few years ago, there was this convention-type thing for mom bloggers. I went. I was scared out of my mind and stayed in bed basically the entire first day because of anxiety and overwhelm, and because the fluorescent lighting gave me a migraine. But I eventually went.

I'm sure some people went there to learn stuff, but let me be quite frank in admitting that I skipped each and every seminar to hang out with people, and that's okay because this wasn't high school, and there were no tardy slips or principals, so . . . I did what I wanted like the fully grown adult woman that I am.

On day two, I did get dressed and show up to sit through some lectures and classes. I had every intention of attending. I even got there early, which is a huge deal for me. I'm more of a "sneak in the back ten minutes late, but it's okay because I brought donuts" kind of gal, but as I was waiting for them to unlock the doors, my friend Mary Katherine called me with a dilemma.

"Amy, do you wanna come meet me down in the lobby and go to Nordstrom? I hate my dress. I feel ugly, and I just want something pretty to wear for the awards tonight in case I win and have to go onstage. Pretty please. You don't have to, but my surgery is next week, and I really just want to have fun tonight. PS: I'm drinking a mimosa right now if you want me to order one for you."

MK was having a double mastectomy to remove breast cancer in less than a week, and she lives across the country from me, so my answer was obvious. I was going to soak in every second I could with her. Do not threaten me with a good time. Ever.

"Umm absolutely, I do. Call the Uber, girl. We're going shopping."

We missed everything that day. Every meeting, every seminar. We missed the key speakers, and we missed out on grab bags and getting sponsors and all that, but my word, we had the absolute best time. Zero regrets. All the praise hands for playing hooky. (Unless you're reading this and you're still in school. Then I absolutely do not recommend it. Go to class, and I lied before. Math is the best. Yay algebra! Yay for equations and formulas and numbers! I use these things every single day. They are very important to your future.)

MK found a beautiful dress and tried on some things that were truly horrendous—a lime-green, jeweled number with a keyhole and a sparkly train comes to mind. I ended up buying a dress off the clearance rack for myself, too, because when in Rome, you get the gown marked 80 percent off without even thinking.

I didn't want to go to the awards that night.

In fact, I'd already RSVP'd a big, fat "nope."

I was being bratty and pissy because I didn't get nominated. I felt a little bit like a loser for not having my name on one single ballot and a little bit bitter for not being put up for one single category. I just didn't want to be there. It was like salt in an open wound. Again, this was just another place where I didn't belong.

After a very long Uber ride back to the hotel, in which I became instant best friends with our driver:

Me. *(gets into the car)* Hey! We are headed to the Omni Hotel, please.

(time skip)

Me. *(exiting the car)* I'm gonna be saying a prayer for your surgery next week, Casey, or should I call you Case? Whatever you prefer. God's got this. God's got you, and you tell your sister that she needs to dump that guy. She's too good for him. If I know anything, it's that she deserves so much better than Jason. He's such a creep. Okay, bye. Call me and tell me how everything goes.

I said goodbye to everyone and told them I was heading in for the night. I wished Mary Katherine good luck and told her how proud I was whether she won or not. I gave out hugs and swore I was fine.

"No, of course I'm not sad, and I'm definitely not jealous. I just hate getting dressed up, and I hate fancy food, and they probably don't even have a seat for me anymore anyway."

But I was a little jealous.

Not ugly jealous, but natural jealous.

It's normal to feel jealous. It's normal to be let down when someone else receives something you wanted. It's normal. It's also normal to compare and to compete, but that doesn't mean these things are good. It doesn't mean they're healthy, and it doesn't mean it's okay to act on any of those feelings. Ugly feelings can quickly turn to ugly actions, and ugly actions can quickly turn to ugly relationships.

Feelings happen, and that's okay. They deserve a space on our journey, but they don't necessarily deserve to sit in the driver's seat on the way to every destination. Sometimes you've gotta tell them to take a hike.

So that's what I did, and I am so grateful because it turned out to be an amazing night.

I finally came to the conclusion that, no, I couldn't control whether I was nominated for any awards, and I couldn't control who won, but I was 100 percent in control of my night. I wasn't a terrified, timid little girl anymore. I wasn't overcome with self-doubt and self-pity. I wasn't afraid to walk into that room with my head held high and a smile on my face, even if I had to sit on the floor.

I couldn't be the girl who left with a trophy, but I could be the girl who cheered the loudest, celebrated her friends the hardest, and had the most fun, so I slipped on my pink chiffon dress with the gold foil design. I clipped in my fake ponytail, and I glued on some fake eyelashes, and I grabbed my set of tiny hands because nothing says fancy night like plastic tiny hands from Amazon. I bragged to everyone who would listen about how cheap my dress was. I met as many people as possible, and I whooped it up Tag Team—style when Mary Katherine walked away with the highest honor of the night.

I didn't get a trophy, but I did win in every way possible.

My jealousy quickly faded into celebration for my friend. My fears of inadequacy gave way to the freedom to simply be myself and enjoy the night. My selfish heart melted into a puddle of camaraderie and togetherness, and I learned so much.

❦

I'll never miss out on an opportunity to celebrate others in a major way because cheering for people is one of the single greatest joys in life. It's fun to cheer for our friends. It's fun to clap for our family. It's even fun to compliment, praise, and boost up complete strangers. We should all do these things more. I'll never let jealousy hold me back from a good time. I'll never let comparison and competition stand in the way of a good friendship, and I'll never go back to that high school cafeteria. I'll never step foot in there again.

I'll never allow myself to hide away or to believe that I have to be someone else to fit in. I'll never force my way in, and I won't squeeze myself in just to claim a seat at the "it" table. I won't blend in, and I won't shy away. I absolutely will never believe that there isn't plenty of room for each and every beautiful one of us to thrive and to shine and to come alive in the most glorious way possible.

You're not the same girl you used to be either.

You've cried too many tears, and you've laughed too many laughs. You've come too far, and you've grown too much to ever go back. You've been through some hard things, and you've come out on the other side still standing. You've survived. You've blossomed. You've become.

You've become someone brand new, so live in a brand-new way, sister.

Live in freedom. Walk in confidence. Talk like a woman who knows who she is and who knows exactly the kind of calling she was created for. Act like you were created this way on purpose.

Do not be discouraged, and don't doubt your ability to plant some amazing flowers because of someone else's green grass. Don't push other women out; hold them close. Don't look at them as competition; look at them as inspiration.

You're a grown-up. This is your one and only beautiful, messy, wild, mild, and crazy life—your life. Don't waste a second wondering where you belong and if you belong, and worrying that people won't make a spot for you. Don't waste your energy on nonsense. Don't waste your breath thinking that tearing somebody else down could ever bring you higher, and don't waste your God-given calling trying to compete.

We really can all win, and we really can all make it to the finish line. We can all have our moment, and we can all sing our own songs. We can all have a little bit of the spotlight.

We can do this better.

We can do this together.

What Now?

Stop obsessing, stressing, and sulking, and go celebrate someone else. Start being the loudest cheerleader in the stands. Be outspokenly proud of everyone in your life that's growing tall. Learn to separate your feelings from truth, and always let truth win.

Refuse to be the kind of woman who cuts others down before they've had the chance to blossom, and refuse to be the kind of woman who pulls the ladder out from someone else so you can get ahead.

Remember that she can win in her life and you can win in yours. You aren't enemies. You're not in competition with each other. We all have our own races to run and our own paths to carve—do the best you can in yours, and when you see someone doing their best, take the time to give her a high five. Support her, and never revert back to the high school cafeteria again.

11

WHEN YOU'RE A BAD FRIEND

love, Jess

Confession time:

1. I've never successfully shaved my legs in my whole life. That sounds like an exaggeration, but the cute little dress I wore to my friend's wedding assures you it is not. I always think, *This is the time I got it all, I know it!* Two hours later, I find a patch on my calf that looks like it's been growing since the debut of "Jenny from the Block."

2. I stay up way too late because it's the only time my house is

quiet and no one asks me for a bite of whatever I'm eating. Am I going to be grumpy in the morning? Yes. Should I sleep more? Yes. Should I keep watching *Bridgerton* until two in the morning while snacking on cheese? My heart says *yes*.

3. I dip fancy food in ranch dressing. I am who I am.

4. My husband says I do not change the toilet paper rolls. I blame the kids. This has been an ongoing feud where I've taken the time to take actual pictures of said changed rolls to send to him while he's at work. Do I *always* change them? Always is kind of extreme in my opinion, but between you and me, I will continue to blame my children until my last breath.

5. The other day my friend asked me if she could dig in my purse for lip balm. She did not find lip balm, but she did pull out a fully intact McDonald's cheeseburger.

6. I don't like the beloved movie trilogy *The Lord of the Rings*. I know, I'm sorry. If you lose all respect for me, I understand. But please just know I have put in the effort. I have given it at least seven tries, and each time I'm reminded that I just don't really like goblins or rings that much.

Phew, now that we got that out of the way . . .

One more thing: sometimes I'm a bad friend.

I'm just guessing here, but I bet sometimes you are too.

It's important to own that. I'm not saying to dig up some shame. I'm not saying get down on yourself at all. I'm saying, let's normalize the fact that we mess up. Let's normalize the fact that sometimes we're the problem. Let's normalize the fact that we're a bunch of imperfect people learning and just doing our best. Honestly, it's the absolute best place to start.

The truth is that if perfection is the standard for friendship, then not a single one of us will measure up.

One time, Aubree and I went to the thrift store. We were both exhausted, and our kids were acting like drunk college students. We spent half the time crawling on our hands and knees trying to retrieve them out from under the clothing racks. The other half was spent breaking up fights over a rocking horse without a head.

Somewhere in the middle of kid-ageddon, my friend pulled out a high chair that had seen better days. "Hey," she said, "can I get this and leave it at your house for the baby when we come over?"

I imagined it sitting in my kitchen all red and yellow and plasticky.

"I don't want that," I said with the intensity one might expect if she had just offered me crack cocaine. I pulled a naked Barbie out of my daughter's mouth.

"Why not?" she said.

"I don't want that at my house."

"How about the garage?"

"It's full."

She squinted at me as we both visualized my garage that could probably fit two hundred of those exact high chairs along with a couple of four-wheelers and maybe even a half-pipe. I squinted back at her, daring her to question my assessment of the space.

"Okayyyyy," she said, noticeably irritated. She shoved it back.

We barely made it out of that place alive. As soon as we had the children strapped down, we had one of our first real fights.

About a high chair. An oversized, red-and-yellow high chair. Our kids even asked us to stop fighting as they ate french fries off the ground.

At one point I yelled, "It was ugly and I hated it!"

Her eyebrows touched her hairline. "It would have fit in your garage if you wanted it to!"

We like to fondly refer to it as the Thrift Store Fight of 2016.

Friendship is messy and sometimes we're total jerkwads. I was a jerkwad. I'll admit it. I had a bad attitude and probably needed a coffee and a better iron supplement. She hadn't slept in eight months because of the baby and was pretty much over taking anyone's crap. That day the crap was mine, and she wasn't having it. Now we laugh about it because—can we be real? Everyone is ridiculous sometimes.

The thing is that when you get close (like really close), you also get up close and personal to each other's "real." That sounds all cutesy and nice on paper, but "real" isn't just wearing your sweats around each other and talking about your sex lives. It's also being raw and unfiltered and sometimes making mistakes. Sometimes "real" is code for "yikes." I wake up on the regular looking like I got punched in the face by my pillow. That fact alone should set the stage for the rest of my life.

Most of us are just hangin' on by a thread. Our schedules are overpacked, our emotions are overrun, and it feels like the most we can do is fall into the couch at night and watch a show or browse Instagram. It's a lot. We're trying to manage too many things already. Friendship can easily feel like one more thing.

The way forward is lots of grace for our limitations and conviction to do our best.

Don't give up just because you can't be perfect. When I was in high school, my organization style was "keep shoving it in there until you can't shove anymore." My locker got so full of papers, books, and things that smelled weird that I just stopped using it and started using my friend's instead (which I'm pretty sure she did not love, now that I think about it). I had to wade through clothing, *People* magazines, and empty Maybelline Great Lash mascara tubes to go in my bedroom, so I started sleeping on the couch (until my mom told me I must face my fear of the mugs under my bed that were growing things and sleep in the actual bed they had provided for me). Later in life, I realized that it was all or nothing for me. If I cleaned my room it was *perfect*, but as soon as a singular sock dropped on the floor, I gave up and didn't try at all.

I've grown out of that now (for the most part), but I think it's easy to look at friendship in the same way: all or nothing, amazing or nada, the perfect friend or "I just won't try." The problem is that we see this idealistic way of being a "good friend" and it feels like too dang much. We're too tired. We're too busy. We're too swallowed up by our schedules to be some sort of rock-star friend.

Let me set the record straight: being a good friend does not mean being a perfect friend. It doesn't mean always knowing the right thing to say or do. It doesn't mean sacrificing all your needs to make someone else happy. It doesn't mean never feeling awkward or unsure. It doesn't mean being available day or night, 24-7. Being a good friend means being intentional about giving *what you can*. It means showing up whenever possible. It means texting to check in when your week is too crazy to get together.

It means loving right smack dab in the middle of the mess and chaos.

Do yourself a favor (and your friends a favor too): don't wait until you can be perfect because that's never going to happen. Show up now. Instead of waiting until you can go on a girls' weekend trip, get happy hour on a Sunday evening. Instead of waiting till you can buy her an extravagant gift, grab a card or a latte to leave on the porch. Instead of waiting until you have five hours to talk on the phone, call while you're commuting and let her know you have twenty minutes but just want to hear her voice. Instead of waiting till you can have her over for dinner, invite her to join you on a grocery shopping trip to Costco. Instead of waiting until life slows down, connect whenever you can.

We have to do whatever we can, and we can't afford to wait.

The closer you are, the more likely you are to screw up. When you are casual friends, you can mostly behave. You can pretend to be in a good mood when you're PMSing. You can smile and hide it when you're really having the worst day. You can keep the crazy tucked away to save for your spouse when you get home (lucky them). When you get really close to your friends, the crazy starts to leak through the cracks—kinda like my extra boob skin leaks out the bottom of my swimsuit sometimes (special thanks to breastfeeding). The good news is that one of the greatest gifts of friendship is to know and be known. There's not a single one of us who doesn't have flaws. There's not a single one of us who isn't gonna screw up sometimes, but every single time you weather a storm of messing up and making it right, your friendship grows stronger.

I'm not going to sugarcoat it. It's painful to be really known sometimes. It's scary to let people be close enough that they become familiar with your flaws and the face you make when you're grumpy. It's painful; it's scary; but it's also a relief. I love that I don't have to edit or filter myself around my closest friends and that I'm okay to just be me. I'm also okay with the reality that my friends are going to mess up sometimes too. They're going to hurt my feelings. They're going to let me down. We're people; that's what we do. I'm going to fail, and they're going to fail, but the safety comes in the fact that we're not going anywhere when we do. We're going to keep showing up even when we make a big ole stink with our bad attitudes and say, "I'm sorry I was a total weirdo today, and I'm sorry I hurt your feelings. I probably could have squeezed it in my giant garage."

The key is that when we make a mess, we have to show back up to the mess and clean it up.

I don't think we leave enough room for failure in our relationships. If you're in any long-term relationship with anyone, you are going to fail. We need to change the conversation from "not failing" to what to do when we do fail. So what steps should we take to clean up the messes we make? Walk with me for a minute.

Step #1: Stay

Your friendship is bigger than most obstacles.

As a society, we are deep in "cancel culture," and can I be honest? It's toxic. There aren't second chances or giving people the benefit of the doubt. It's one strike and you're out. One misstep and bye, see ya later. We do it to celebrities; we do it to public figures; and worst of all, we do it to friends and family.

Listen, we can't ever build deep friendships if that is our mentality. That's like offering someone a tightrope without a net. *Hi, you can be my friend, but* don't mess up, *'cause if you do, girl, bye.*

If we're going to be good friends, we need to go counter-cultural and create a safe space. We need to leave room to be hurt. We need to leave room to do the hurting. We need to leave room to make mistakes. We need to leave room for failure (both theirs and ours). We need to leave room to take a flipping breath and let our hair down. This isn't a performance, and it's not a test.

This is about belonging to each other in a way that's not easily breakable.

To be clear: I'm not talking about staying in a toxic or abusive relationship, but I am talking about doing hard things for the sake of friendships that are worth the fight.

Step #2: Head Straight for the Fire

If you smell smoke, don't ignore it; find out what's going on before it burns down the whole house.

A few months back, I hurt a friend completely unintentionally. She was going through something really hard, and she felt like I'd taken a step back instead of being present while she was struggling. Things had felt weird between us, so I sent her a text and asked, "Hey are we good?" She was brave enough to respond, "I don't know, I'm feeling hurt right now." I dropped everything I was doing, called to my husband that I would be back, and drove straight to her house.

I let myself in and went to find her. She was sitting cross-legged on the floor folding laundry. I sat down across from her, plopped down my keys, grabbed a T-shirt to start folding, and said, "Okay, what's going on?"

The tears streamed down her face as she told me how alone she'd been feeling and how it felt like I'd pulled away.

The truth was, I hadn't pulled away on purpose. I just hadn't known what she needed, and I assumed what she needed was some space. I told her I was so sorry, and we sat there on the floor listening to each other. She cried, and I cried. I hadn't intentionally hurt my friend, but that didn't change the fact that I'd hurt her. I needed to sit with that. I needed to sit and listen and really hear her. I needed to tell her I understood and I would do things differently next time.

Step #3: Clean Up Your Mess; Make It Right

When you make a mess, don't let shame make you hide. Don't let defensiveness keep you from being soft and open. Don't brush it under the carpet like a ten-thousand-pound elephant 'cause, spoiler alert: it doesn't go away. To have close friendships, we need to clean up our messes. Maybe it was an accident, or maybe you did something that was just plain ugly. Either way, don't pull away. Sit on the floor and listen. Hash it out. Clean up your mess.

Sometimes I walk into my kitchen in the morning in a pre-coffee stupor and discover that my nighttime self forgot to clean up the dinnertime explosion that occurred feeding my four kids (my four kids who also apparently thought it was a good idea to start a craft on top of the petrified spaghetti noodles first thing in the morning). Nothing like glitter and a Mount Kilimanjaro of dishes to start my day. It occurs to me in that moment that it would probably be easier and faster to burn the whole thing down, but because I'm an adult and also because my husband tends to frown on house fires, I wade in one crusty fork at a time. *Eventually*, after several shots of espresso and some elbow grease, my kitchen emerges from the garbage pile, and it turns out it is still fully functional.

When we make a mess in our friendships it's tempting to pull away and move on. It can be overwhelming when we confront the mistakes we've made, but gosh, friendships are so precious, and they're not disposable. They're worth every single second we spend cleaning up after ourselves.

We've just got to wade in, one crusty fork at a time.

Step #4: Be Real About Your Own Hurt Feelings and Forgive

Sometimes it's even harder to admit you're hurt. If you've ever been a part of any relationship at all, there's a 100 percent guarantee that you've been let down. Just yesterday, I was on the phone with a friend, and I had to put on my big girl pants and say, "Hey, you kind of said 'I told you so' about that decision I made, and it's really been bothering me." Her words had been poking me like an aggravated splinter, even though I'd tried to shake it off.

She had no idea her words had affected me like that. She apologized, I forgave her, and the splinter was gone.

The thing is that it's hard to be vulnerable. It's hard to admit that we're not invincible and that we can be hurt. I have no idea why I've decided it's a good quality to be tough in my relationships, but I've spent so much of my life telling myself things like:

- *It's not a big deal; no one else would be hurt by that.*
- *I'm the problem; I need to get over it.*
- *I'm not hurt; I'm fine. Keep smiling.*
- *Don't let them see me cry.*
- *OMG stop being so dramatic.*

Maybe I didn't leave the room I was in, but my heart sure did. My heart checked out, grabbed my pain, and headed straight out the door. Friend, if you're constantly shushing your feelings, that's no way to do friendship. Friendship is about belonging, and sometimes that means staying in the room and working things out. Sometimes that means taking a deep breath and sharing your most sensitive and broken places.

I'm not suggesting that every time we feel a feeling we put it on our friends like it's their fault. That's not healthy or fun. I'm saying sometimes there's something kinda big that we try to keep small. Instead of that thing going away (like we hoped), it flares up every time something else hurts us. If it keeps flaring, it probably needs to be talked about. When you do, keep it simple, keep it humble, and just be real. You don't need to lawyer up or come in with guns blazing. You don't need to think of a really good way to make your point or start with a heavy accusation. This isn't an intergalactic space battle; it's a conversation between two friends stepping closer to each other instead of farther away.

Step #5: Shake It Off (Ain't Nobody Perfect)

Sister, you can't get everything right (and neither can anyone else); we're not butter.

We have to leave space for failure in our friendships. There has to be room for that, or the whole thing will be either shallow or doomed. Shake it off. Dance it off. Do what you gotta do, and let it go. Friendship is messy, and ultimately, that's a part of its beauty.

I find grace is always circular. If I'm being hard on myself, I'll start being hard on my friends too. If I'm being kind and gentle with myself, I'll be naturally kind and gentle toward my friends.

Don't penny pinch with grace. Give it out in armfuls and truckloads. Every single one of us is broken and full of flaws. You make mistakes. So what? Me too. Let's make a club where everyone belongs.

Sometimes the Damage Is Irreparable—What Then?

Most of us have stories where a friend hurt us. Whether we like it or not, those experiences can define us. People fail us, and sometimes they fail big. Sometimes they fail really, really big. Every single one of us has been hurt by a bad friend. I don't know your stories, but I know you have them. Maybe your wound is still raw and open. Maybe you've been hurt so many times you're just not sure if you can ever trust again.

In high school, I had a friend I was really close to. I'd thrown open the doors to the deepest places in my heart and invited her to cozy up on the couch and stay. I trusted her completely, and she was a constant part of my life. I believed in her with my whole heart, and when other people tried to tell me that maybe things weren't as they seemed, I was her fierce defender.

A few years into our friendship, the lies she was trying to hold together began to unravel, slowly at first, and then all at once like an unexpected hurricane. It came crashing down around me when I found out everything she'd ever told me was a lie. The situation is hard to explain without giving details I can't give, but in short, she'd taken advantage of me, she'd manipulated me, and she'd stolen from me. Overnight, she went from being one of my most trusted people to being a person I barely knew, and it shook me. It shook me to my core. It wasn't so much what she did; it was the hours we'd spent sharing our hearts, crying together, and laughing together that suddenly were fake and empty.

This was nearly two decades ago now, and I don't blame her or have hard feelings toward her. She just wasn't healthy enough to be a good friend, and I know (now) it had nothing to do with me at all. But to be honest, it took me a minute. I honestly felt deep grief. It came in big waves of anger, hurt, and just plain sadness.

Sister, part of moving on with a free heart into new friendships is forgiving and releasing. I know it's hard, and sometimes it takes time. I heard once that unforgiveness is like chaining yourself to that person forever. It doesn't affect them at all, but it affects you. It weighs you down and follows you into every single new friendship, or it keeps you from risking in any new relationships at all. If you have pain like that, I get it. I'm so sorry you've gone through that.

Can I say something in the gentlest way possible? If you haven't let it go, it might be time. It might be time to release it and let your heart heal all the way. It might be time to tell that pain that it doesn't need to protect you anymore; you're ready to let it go.

Life is uncertain, and I can't make any promises, but I can tell you I risked again, and it was worth it. It was worth it a million times over. I have friends now who are loyal and tell the truth. Are they perfect? Of course not, but they're just exactly what my heart needed. Sometimes we are the bad friend, and sometimes we are the brunt of a bad friend. Sometimes the friendship is worth the fight, and sometimes it's time to let it go. The important thing is that we don't give up. There is always hope, even if it doesn't come in the package we expected.

What Now?

If you're ready, write a letter of forgiveness to someone (maybe that someone is you). This is for your eyes only (it isn't something you're ever going to send). Make it as raw and real as your heart needs. I'll go first.

Dear _____,

I forgive you.

You hurt me, and it sucked. What you did wasn't okay,

and forgiving you doesn't say that it was. I felt like my heart was shattered by your betrayal, and I felt that for a long time. But I forgive you, and I release you. I'm not going to carry this around anymore; I'm letting it go.

Love,

_____

Once you've written your letter, give yourself a minute, and then trash it. Toss it in the fire, run it through the paper shredder, cut it into itty-bitty pieces, make it into a wad and shoot a two pointer into the wastebasket. It doesn't matter what you do with it; what matters is that that ship has sailed, that water is under the bridge, that door is shut, and the only thing in front of you is wide-open space and a future full of new stories.

Five Friendship Revelations

1. *They're not you.* If you get one thing from this book, let it be this: other people are not you. They don't think like you. They don't feel like you. They don't care about the same things you care about, and they will not respond the same way you would respond. We can't manipulate or force them into our boxes. That will only exhaust us, make us incredibly anxious, and drive a massive wedge between us. We have to allow people the freedom to do life their way. Yes, this makes relationships infinitely trickier, but it also makes them infinitely more interesting, fun, and beautiful.

2. *You'll always find what you're looking for.* Listen up. If you expect people to reject you, fail you, or be mean and hurtful, you're going to find what you're looking for. If you walk through life thinking, *There's no one out there who isn't catty and petty*, guess what you're going to find? If the problem follows you around to every relationship you have, chances are it's a *you* problem, not a *them* problem, and there isn't a single friend who can fix this for you. Learn to look for the good—really, really look for it—and you're most likely going to find what you're looking for.

3. *Awkwardness is normal when you're making new friends.* Sweaty palms? Itchy neck? Talking too much? Unable to think of *literally anything* to say? Wondering if you're weird and then coming to the conclusion that, yep, you're definitely weird? All normal. When you're getting to know someone, it is awkward. We used to think it was because we were doing something wrong, but then our friends shared that they felt

the same way. How validating! So go into a new friendship expecting it to be kinda weird at first. Just because someone is hard to get to know doesn't mean they aren't worth getting to know, and just because the relationship is uncomfortable at first doesn't mean it will stay uncomfortable.

4. *You are not the center of anyone else's universe.* If you're anything like us, you pretend to know what other people are thinking and feeling. Our minds can get the best of us, and we start to believe that because we weren't invited to something, there must have been some plot to hurt us. Or if someone is overly kind and inclusive, they must be plotting ways to bring us down. The truth is, most people probably aren't thinking about us at all. While we're questioning people's intentions, they are questioning what to make for dinner. The truth is, we are not the center of anyone else's world. We're secondary characters in everyone else's books at best, and that's okay. That's the way it is supposed to be.

5. *A pure heart sleeps well.* You can say all the right things and still have those words be taken out of context. People can reject you even when you've been nothing but kind. You can be straight-up sunshine in the flesh and people can still paint you in ugly colors. You can give it your very best and still have it go very badly. You can try, but that doesn't mean your efforts will always be enough. I (Amy) have learned that I can control what I do, but I can't control the way people feel about me. Every night, I kiss my husband, turn the fan on high, say my prayers, and ask myself this one question: *Was my heart pure?* And if I can honestly say that my heart was in the right place, I can sleep easy.

12

When You've Been There, Done That, and Had Your Heart Break

Love, Amy

I don't know why I'm writing this chapter.

Probably because Jess is a true optimist, enthusiast, and the most anti-negative human on the face of this planet, and she stuck me with it. Typical. Thanks, Jess.

I've never been through a friend breakup.

And yes, thank you for asking, it is really hard balancing that many best friends. Nobody ever asks, so that means a lot to me. Replying to texts alone is a full-time job.

It's exhausting and overwhelming. I am so popular.

I'm kidding.

I have friends—I actually have amazing friends—but I only have like one friend I hang out with on a regular basis, and I mostly just text my mom. I plan a girls' night every six months that typically either gets canceled or is over by nine o'clock because we're all way too tired, and sadly, I've definitely been through my fair share of friend breakups. Possibly because I'm a mess and because I divulge all of my deepest feelings and diary entries on the internet regularly like a weirdo.

Who wouldn't want to be my friend?! I am delightful.

But it happens.

Friendships break. Friendships rip, and they shift, and they lose their strength from time to time. They end, and they tear, and they leave you wondering why. What happened, what you could've done differently, and how someone could ever treat you that way. They leave you speechless and breathless and confused and hurt. They fracture, they drift, they evolve, and they dissolve. They go slowly, and sometimes they sprint out of the building and out of sight before you even know what's happened.

The older I get, the more I realize the thing I crave most in my life is stability—stability, comfort, and low-carb snacks that don't taste like feet. Some people love change. I am not some people.

I want everyone good in my life to stay in my life. And I want a fair warning before the rug gets pulled from under my feet.

I want promises that nobody is going to change their minds or go anywhere. No curveballs when it comes to my people. I want consistency, constancy, and promises. Promises that we're going to give it all we have to make it work for the long haul. Loyalty as well as sustainability and dependability. Please also get my jokes and always think I'm funny. Seriously. That's all I ask.

But the older I get, the more I become acutely aware that not much in life is promised. I think that's why being an adult is so hard. Bills kind of stink, and your obligations get heavier, and suddenly all the really good food gives you heartburn. (Thanks, pizza.) So there's that, but you are also slapped with this harsh reality that things change, and people change too. With every candle that gets added to my birthday cake, I realize more and more that I never had as much control over things as I thought I did. I've realized that people are beautiful but complicated, and we are all magnificently woven together, so we should dance like crazy every single chance we get because they weren't lying when they said life is short.

Outside of God's love, there aren't a ton of guarantees.

My parents got divorced after twenty-seven years of marriage. That hit me a bit by surprise, but that's life. It changes in an instant. Sometimes it changes in the most beautiful way possible: a new career, an unexpected opportunity, a newfound love. Sometimes it brings you to your knees: a call, an accident, a diagnosis, a loss.

Sometimes even the most solid of friendships crumble like a piece of fragile notebook paper. Sometimes there's a reason. Sometimes there isn't. Sometimes trust is broken. Sometimes we don't listen to each other. Sometimes we refuse to understand each other. Sometimes things have gone straight-up toxic and we need out. Sometimes we just aren't as like-hearted as we thought we once were, and there's no common thread to hold us together anymore.

For every million breakups, there are a million different reasons why.

I don't know anyone who's been excused from the hurt of a relationship gone wrong. I didn't know that for a long time. For a long time, I thought I was the only one. With every fiber of my being, I thought there must be something deeply and inherently wrong with who I was for people to leave me, like maybe I was defective. Or maybe my personality was kind of like a Monet painting—from far away, I looked really good, was fun and easygoing, but the closer you got, the more it became apparent that I was just a bunch of messy dots. Or even worse, maybe I was lake water where things looked fine on the surface, but as you dived deeper you realized there was trash and mildew and seaweed lined all along the bottom.

I always assumed I was actively repulsive. Sometimes I'd forget to put on deodorant, so maybe that was the problem. I felt alone on this island—alone and embarrassed, and then I read Lysa TerKeurst's *Uninvited*, which is about feeling rejected and less than and alone. When she talked about losing a friend, my mind was 100 percent blown.

Whhhhhhat? Who wouldn't want to be Lysa's friend? I want to be Lysa's friend. What is even going on here? I couldn't begin to wrap my mind around it. I figured people like her, people as successful and beautiful and talented and put-together as Lysa, must have everyone clawing at their doors trying to get the chance just to know them. Surely, she had a massive pile of invitations sitting on her kitchen counter that she was too busy to even answer. Surely.

But no. It turns out, she was kind of like me, and when I read that book, I exhaled for the first time in a long time. Maybe I was going to be okay. Maybe I was going to have good friendships after all, and maybe these breakups were simply a part of life—not only my life, but every woman's life.

Maybe my best friend in high school didn't wake up one day and decide to hate me after ten long years of being inseparable after all. Maybe she just needed to pull away and go in a different direction. Maybe she was just trying to grow up, and that's the only way she knew how.

Maybe those friends who broke up with me in a note had no idea how that would leave me shattered for years. Looking back, it only made sense. Those friends had lives that were completely different from mine. They had serious boyfriends. They were about to graduate, get jobs, and get married. Their lives were sunshine. Meanwhile, I was smack-dab in the middle of a Category 5 hurricane, so I kept them at a distance from everything going on with me.

I hid away, and I lied, and I wore a pretty thick mask so they couldn't see the truth. I was a horrible friend. I was so focused on my own storms and so consumed with my own problems, I didn't know how to celebrate the good things happening in their lives.

These were not bad people. These were really, really good people—people who were only doing what was best for them. I blamed myself, but I never once blamed them for leaving. I was the one looking for answers to dark questions in the wrong places. I was the one searching for something steady in a stream of bad decisions. I was the one who was faltering, and that's not their fault.

Without diving too deep into it, I had been through some major trauma, and I was so ashamed. Something like that was never supposed to happen to someone like me. I'd always been the good girl. I'd always done things right. I'd always lived by this certain checklist, this code, and it had all been washed away in an instant by someone else's carelessness.

I had these major holes, and I tried to fill them up with anything I could find. I tried to fill them up with going out, with working out, with losing weight, with looking a certain way, with dating—so much dating. I thought maybe if I could find the right guy, I could move forward and forget about all of it. I thought the trauma would be erased. Turns out, it doesn't work like that.

I didn't tell my friends anything. I didn't tell anyone anything. I didn't want to tarnish a mostly golden reputation with all this junk, so I tried to ignore it.

When they moved on, it left a wound like I couldn't even begin to explain. I didn't think anyone would ever want me again, and I believed their walking away was only more proof that this was the way things would always be for me.

Thank goodness Jesus' arms are wide and his heart has plenty of room for all of us. Thank goodness that even at my smallest, he was big enough to save a wretch, a mess, and a little lost soul like mine. Thank goodness for that cross, and thank goodness for therapists too.

I wish I'd gotten help sooner. I wish I'd known I didn't have to do it alone, and I wish I hadn't tried so hard to carry all those bags on my own. I wish I'd known there was zero shame in finding a professional to help me sift through everything. I wish I'd known how many resources were available.

And do you know what else I wish?

I wish I'd realized that you can't heal something you refuse to admit is broken in the first place.

﹀

Through these friend breakups, I learned a lot. I learned a lot about myself and about others. I learned a lot about what to do and what not to do when you're in the midst of this kind of heartbreak. And about what you can do to get to the other side. Here are ten of those things I'd like to share with you:

1. *Friend breakups are hard, so give yourself permission to feel.* For whatever reason, I think women tend to stay relatively hush-hush about the pain they've experienced from a friendship that didn't go the way they'd hoped. Maybe it's because we're embarrassed things didn't work out, or maybe it's because "some people have it so much worse" and we feel guilty for complaining, or maybe we think it's stupid that we're upset about the situation at all. I don't know, honestly, but I do know that the more we keep these things to ourselves, the more we tend to believe the lie that we are the only ones who have ever walked this path. Don't you dare feel guilty if you feel gutted. Don't you dare feel shame if it takes you some time to get over it. A friend breakup is a loss after all, and losses are always to be grieved. Nobody gets to tell you how to do it, how to feel, or how many tears you're allowed to cry. It hurts. Whether you left or they left or it was completely mutual; no matter when it happened or how it happened—it hurts, and that's okay.

2. *Do things out of love, not desperation.* I am all for loving people well. I'm all for loving people big. I'm all for

making sure people know how you feel about them. I am not, however, in favor of begging, bugging, manipulating, guilting, chasing, or clinging. If someone needs space and wants to walk away from the friendship, please show them the door with grace and some self-respect. You're not a doormat. You're not desperate. You're disappointed.

3. *Bitterness is never the answer.* Like I said earlier, it's okay to feel hurt over a friendship breakup. It's okay to be sad and to grieve and to wish it had ended differently. Or, actually, to wish it hadn't ended at all. It's okay if you're mad, and it's okay if your feelings are dinged up a bit. It's one thing to feel anger, but it's another thing to live in anger. Make sure bitterness doesn't make its way into all those little cracks and take root. It grows rapidly and wildly, and it spreads quickly. Bitterness is not a good home, and there is no warmth in resentment. Do your best to get to a place where you can release a person who wasn't made for you without hating them, villainizing them, or running them down behind their back. This is maturity. A friendship ending does not require drama, and it does not necessarily make the two of you active enemies.

4. *Forgiveness is pretty good for everyone.* I always thought God asked us to forgive because it was best for the other person, and he did. When he asked us to love our neighbors, I have to believe that forgiving them was automatically built into the equation. People are human. They will do human things. You will do human things. I will do human things. None of us will get through without forgiveness. Forgiveness doesn't excuse bad behavior, and

it doesn't ignore the wrong that incurred, but it does set things free. With age and (hopefully) wisdom, I understand that forgiveness is every bit as much for my own heart as it is for the other person's. It gives us both wings to be released and to move forward. Whether we move forward together or separately, at least we'll have the freedom to fly. Unforgiveness will make you want revenge on the person. Forgiveness will make you want to pray for the person. There is more peace to be found in praying.

5. *Shaming and blaming won't help you grow.* Blaming is so tempting, and pointing the finger is so enticing. Pushing full responsibility on the other party makes it significantly easier to push our pain away. The more we peddle the fault fully on them, the more we avoid our own responsibility for the way things went down. But there's always another side to the story, and there's almost always something we could have done differently. Blaming is a barrier to understanding others, understanding our own mistakes, and understanding how to make relationships function as well as possible. Straight-up, blaming simply doesn't work, and it doesn't benefit anyone—not them and not you.

6. *There are things to learn here—valuable things.* Maybe you learn about yourself. Maybe you learn about other people. Maybe you learn about the things you do well and the areas where you lack. Maybe you learn about boundaries. Maybe you learn about the things you need in a friendship. Maybe you learn about the importance of apologies or the significance of words. Maybe you

learn how to let things go. Maybe you learn how to give. Maybe you learn how to pull back. Maybe you learn about confidence, and you learn to speak to yourself with more kindness. I don't know exactly what you'll learn. It is unique for each of us, and it is unique for each situation, but you'll learn something; and the hope is that those things serve as fuel to bring you into the next friendship stronger, smarter, more proficient, more efficient, and significantly healthier.

7. *Hold your integrity tight.* You lost the relationship, but that doesn't mean you need to lose yourself. Remember who you are and what you believe. Stand on truth, and secure yourself to a strong set of morals. Get through this with your head held high and your heart beaming with purity. You have woven things like love and light and loyalty and goodness and kindness and self-control into the fabric of your life for a long time. You have worked mercilessly at becoming a woman you are proud of. Do not lose these things when a friendship unravels. This trial will not be your undoing. It will only serve to reveal your truest self—and I, for one, believe your truest self is solid gold, baby.

8. *Don't bring your old crap into a new house.* One of the worst things you can do for a new relationship is to walk through the door carrying all the suitcases, duffel bags, and tote bags full of junk from the old relationship. Don't assume that this friendship will end the same way the other friendship ended. Don't assume anything. This isn't the same friendship, and this isn't the same person. Don't

wrap yourself in your old hurts and think they will keep you warm. Give it a chance, and erase all of the old markings from the chalkboard. Start fresh.

9. *Sometimes things come back around.* Once in a while, friendships circle around like a boomerang. They work their way back like a tacky trend from the eighties, and things work out on the second shot. It's beautiful when they do. Sometimes old wounds have been repaired, and both people have learned from their mistakes. Sometimes life simply brings you two together again. Schedules have changed, and timelines have changed, and suddenly you're in the same place at the same time looking for the same thing. Sometimes the weirdness from before makes the relationship even stronger. If the relationship was mostly good—if there is something to be saved and revived— save, revive, and reconnect.

10. *And sometimes they don't, but that's okay too.* And then again, sometimes closed doors stay closed. Sometimes cars that have shut down never run again, and sometimes friendships that have broken up remain in pieces. That's okay. Some relationships were meant to remain a memory, pictures in an old scrapbook that you can look back and smile on from time to time. Try to be grateful if you can because the emptiness it left in its wake also means that there's a blank space just waiting to be filled. Fill it with new people. Fill it with new opportunities. Fill it with new hobbies. Fill it with new adventures and a new outlook. Fill it with a new attitude, and fill it with so much faith.

Now, years later, after some hard and heartbreaking friend breakups, I look at my husband—my good, good husband—and my three gorgeous children, and I just smile. Sure, I miss those old friends sometimes. Once in a while, I scroll past their pictures on Facebook, and I wish I'd gotten to go to their weddings. I wish I knew their kids, and I wish we'd kept in touch, but I don't wish things had transpired any differently.

These were all steps that have brought me to where I am today, and I like where I'm standing. I would never want to be anywhere else, and I do believe God used all those ashes from my past to bring about some beautiful things today.

Even so, sometimes I still wish I could go back and encourage the old me. I wish I could show her a glimpse of the goodness that was about to unfold, and I wish I could be there for her. I wish I could read her a page out of the next chapter, and I wish I could tell her she's enough. She's enough without all the makeup, and she's enough without the boyfriend. She's enough no matter what the number on her jeans says, and she's enough whether she knows exactly where she's going or she's on a little detour. I wish I could slip a necklace around her neck that says, "He's got you," and I wish I could tell her that she won't ever accept good things until she finds the courage to believe she deserves good things.

I wish I could tell her she'll go on to find more friends, and every single friendship will be magnificent and marvelous and meaningful in its own way.

And I wish I could do the same for you, sister.

If you're anything like me, you've tossed and turned and lain awake at night and wondered if you were the only one. You've wondered why you were so easy to leave in the past and if you'll be easy to leave in the next relationship too. You've wondered why other women seem to have this whole friendship thing figured out. You've wondered if your last friendship would be the last friendship, and you've wondered why it failed.

You've prayed, *Dear God, let this be the one that lasts. I don't know if my heart can stand to lose another one.*

You've replayed conversations, and you've run through every scenario, and you've beat yourself up questioning whether there was anything you could've done that would have made even a bit of difference, and that makes me want to wrap you in the warmest hug.

It happens. Life changes, and friendships break, and it hurts when they do.

You're not alone. I think most women are standing in the ring right there with you. I think most women are nodding along, saying, "Yup, me too. Sister, I am with you."

There's no formula for fixing everything, and there's no cure to help curate the perfect friendship. Nobody has it all figured out, and even the most experty of experts gets it wrong sometimes too. There aren't any guarantees, and I get it—that's scary. I wish there were, and I wish I could have been the one to figure them out because that would be helpful. (And also because I'd be *rich*. Maybe not house-in-the-Hamptons rich, but rich enough to buy that little farm I've always wanted with my miniature horse, Tina Ney; my cow, Dairy Styles; and Arillama Grande, who is obviously a llama. Okay, okay. I promise. I'm done.)

(And my chickens, Hennifer Aniston and Chick Jagger. And my donkey Snoop Donk. But for real now, I'll stop.)

I can't promise anything, but I can tell you trying is always the way to go, and people are always worth the effort. Connection is essential, and you'll never know if you don't put yourself out there.

I can tell you that I've been there, and I'll probably be there again, and so will you, but I will never stop fighting for friendship. I'll never stop believing that the two most beautiful gifts God has ever given us are the gift of grace and the gift of one another.

What Now?

A huge part of what makes a friend breakup so difficult to move past—as opposed to a romantic breakup—is that there usually is no clear "it's not you; it's me" kind of talk. On rare occasions, people may clearly say, "This is what you've done to hurt me," or "This is why things can no longer continue," but typically there is no clear conversation as to when things begin, and there is no clear conversation as to when things end. Most of the time, these things are all muddled, undefined, and we are left alone to figure out where things went wrong. The truth is, we may never know when things shifted or why they shifted. This is both painful and confusing as all get-out, but the good news is that although it takes two people to build a friendship, you can get closure all on your own. Here are some tips to help:

1. Journal. Write it all out. Make lists like:
    - The things I loved about my friend
    - The things I did well in this friendship

- What things she did well in this friendship
- How some things could have been better
- Why I am proud of myself
- Some things I will be looking for in my next friendship

2. Answer questions (and make sure you answer them honestly) like:
   - Am I judging my friend unfairly?
   - Why am I having a hard time moving on?
   - What are some things I can learn from this?
   - Have I really forgiven her?
   - Have I really forgiven myself?
   - Have I been venting about the situation or have I been talking poorly about her?

Don't run yourself down, but do assess your own actions. When we own our faults, we not only take away their power but also make it less likely that we'll make the same mistakes twice. This is how we evolve in our friendships. Where did you mess up? What mistakes did you make? What have you learned? What can you do differently in your next friendship? Again, this isn't about criticizing yourself or feeling guilty. This is about equipping yourself so that the next time you get out there, you do it better.

If, after carefully checking your own heart, you decide you owe your friend an apology, my word, be a grown-up and apologize. Tell her you're sorry, but make sure you are doing it with zero expectations. You cannot control her reactions, and she does not owe you anything. Apologize because it's the right thing to do, and apologize because it will help you move forward, but do not do it with the hope that it will suddenly fix everything. Her response is on her. Say your piece so that you can finally have some peace.

If you decide an apology is not in order, remind yourself that friendship breakups happen. They are a part of life. They are a fact. Some things weren't meant to be forever, and that's okay. Remember the relationship for what it was, and remind yourself of all the open doors that lie ahead. Find hope in knowing that you are now more prepared for the next friendship. I genuinely believe that every broken friendship gets us one piece closer to the right friendship.

13

WHEN YOUR MOUTH GETS STICKY AND WORDS GET HARD

love, Jess

Words matter; use them for good.

When I was in second grade, my bangs started halfway back on my head and were an inch thick. It was the trademark look for girls in the nineties whose moms cut their hair at home. We all remember going to school after a bang "trim." One day we could barely see, and then the next day we looked like Lloyd Christmas and our friends thought we were the new girl.

The day my mom decided to let me grow them out was a very

exciting day for me, mostly because my forehead hadn't felt a cool breeze since 1987. We went to the movies to see *The Lion King*, and she pinned them back with an entire can of hairspray and a few squirts of my dad's max-hold hair gel. She left a thin fringe, and it was that day that I knew I was probably going to grow up and be a JCPenney model and marry Charlie from *The Mighty Ducks*. I was gorgeous.

Little did I know that growing out bangs is not for the faint of heart.

Over the following months, my mom plastered my bangs to my head every morning with so much gel that it looked like I'd either recently taken a shower or gotten caught in a freak rainstorm. Every day they stayed put until one o'clock, when the adhesive wore off just in time for PE. Halfway through my first lap around the gym, I could feel them loosen, and then *thwap*; a giant chunk of cemented hair would smack me in the forehead. With each step, they'd bounce back on my head and then, *thwap*, hit me on the forehead again like they were waving at my friends. *Bounce, bounce, thwap, thwap*. It probably lives on in the whole class's memory. "Do you remember how Jessica Cushman's hair used to wave at us during dodgeball?"

One morning my archenemy Libby N, who got chocolate bars in her lunch and took credit for my art projects, sneered across her Elmer's glue bottle at me. "Is this what's in your hair?" she asked. "Why is your hair so greasy? Is it glue? It's like beeswax." I ignored her and continued cutting up my shapes. "Beeeeeeeswax, beeeeeeswax," she sang.

I do not remember a whole lot about second grade except the bang flapping and the beeswax.

It's crazy how words stick with us, isn't it?

You'd think we'd grow out of name calling, but we don't. We probably don't tap someone on the shoulder in the coffee line and say, "Your perfume smells like dead people," but we do whisper about one another. We do pound on our keyboards calling names and making assumptions that aren't rooted in kindness or goodwill. We do talk behind one another's backs. We do avoid conflict with friends by venting about our issue to someone else.

Are your ears burning yet? Because mine are. I'm guilty of it too. It's a whole lot easier to focus on other people's flaws than deal with my own heart issues. It's a whole lot easier to talk smack about someone than to have a conversation with them to figure it out.

We're all grown up, but words are still hard. We can either use our words to build one another up and speak life into one another's identities, or we can be people who use our words to tear others down.

In 2018, IKEA conducted an experiment about the impact of words on plants.[1] For thirty days, two plants received identical light, nutrition, and water. They also received messages through speakers set in their enclosures. But the messages were different: one plant was being bullied with negative commentary, and the other received complimentary messages. After thirty days, the plant that received compliments and encouragement was healthy and thriving, while the plant that was insulted and bullied was noticeably drooping and wilted.

Death and life are in the power of the tongue.

If a plant without emotions or a soul thrives with encouragement, how much more do we?

I have a child who is full of fire. She's the kind of spicy that makes your eyes water when you eat too much of it at once, like when my husband suggested I take a bite of the green stuff (wasabi) and I didn't stop sweating for seven days. She's my lil' wasabi, and I adore her. To be honest, it took way too long for me to find the voice with which she seems to have been born. Sometimes I'm tired, though, and I secretly want to tame her. Sometimes I'd like her to leave the Target toy aisle without hostage negotiations. Sometimes I'd like bedtime to not take a thousand years. Sometimes I'd like to not have an argument about wearing shoes to the grocery store. The thing is, even when it's hard, even when I mess up and lose my temper, and even when I'm so, so tired, every night when I tuck her in, I tell her this: "Let your light shine, and don't ever hide it." I know my words have the power to suppress her wild and fierce spirit or to set her free. I choose the latter.

Every single person has flaws: they have things that we don't agree with, and they do things we think are annoying. Every. Single. One. We have the choice to focus on that or to focus on the beautiful things that make them *them*. We have the power to suppress, and we have the power to set free.

I believe we're all God's creations, and I believe we're all made in his image. I'm pretty sure he's not up there venting to Jesus about how terrible he thinks we all are. I'm pretty sure he's a proud Father who sees the good in us (even when we don't see it), and I'm pretty sure we're supposed to make our conversations about people match his.

Let's be people who call out the gold in people, not the kind who go mining for garbage.

᪻᪻᪻

Conflict is hard, but we can do it.

> We think we're brave until we have to tell someone they hurt
> our feelings.
>
> —ME, YESTERDAY

One of the hardest things to do is admit when we're hurt. It's vulnerable, and it's risky. I know people who will rant till kingdom come about how awful it is that so-and-so did such and such. It's clear the issue is that their feelings are hurt, but they will always punctuate it with, "I mean, I don't care" or "I'm not mad or anything." You know what? It's okay to be hurt, and it's okay to be mad. Sometimes it's brave to admit when you're hurt or mad, and it's definitely brave to share with your friend how you're feeling.

One of the best communication tools I've learned in my friendships is to be honest and not to wait too long. I *don't* mean going in guns blazing with accusations and assumptions about their intentions (that's a quick way to have a blowup and end up more hurt than before). I mean a simple, "Hey, what did you mean when you said that? It seemed like you meant this, and it hurt my feelings" or "Sometimes when you do that, I feel like you don't value our friendship." Often, they had no idea I felt that way and are quick to make it right.

A friend of mine stopped by the other day after a girls' night and said, "Hey, you were joking about that thing last night, and it was painful for me; I'm not ready to laugh about it." I told her

I was so sorry and thanked her for telling me. I can't promise all those conversations will go well. It is a risk to be vulnerable, but there's a very good chance that you will walk away closer than you were before. Deep friendship requires honesty; it requires humility (especially when you're wrong); and it requires heartfelt apologies.

Conflict is going to come up in friendship. At some point, we're going to get our feelings hurt or misunderstand each other, and it's so important that we're able to talk about it.

There's not a single one of us who doesn't have blind spots. Not. A. Single. One. When I'm stressed, I get defensive, and sometimes I wear the same pants too many days and it shows. I interrupt a lot and am not always a good listener, and when I wear a dress without makeup and bring all four kids to the store, I look like I have a special religion. These are all things I've learned from my friends.

Friendship is a safe place for iron to sharpen iron. If we don't stick it out with our friends and we run at the first sign of conflict, how will we grow? If we don't gently tell the truth and constructively call each other out, how will we get closer? We definitely won't grow through gossip, and we certainly won't get close by avoiding hard things.

The path of friendship isn't always through green pastures, along streams, and dancing across hillsides like Maria from *The Sound of Music*. Sometimes, it's through dark forests and muddy waters. Sometimes things are going to get messy, murky, and hard. The thing to remember is that it's an honor to walk through both paths. The depth that comes from walking through the hard places can never be bought any other way.

In Montana, where I used to live, it didn't get hot very often. We used to pull out our flip-flops and cut-off denims on the first sunny day in spring, when the puddles are still frozen over and rich people hadn't yet ventured back from Arizona. Occasionally, we would get a couple of ninety-degree days in the summer, and our houses would feel like the deep Amazonian jungle because no one had air conditioning or fridges with functioning ice cube makers. (My definition of "arriving" in life will be when I have a functioning ice cube maker.) Montanans have very little resilience to heat, so we would all flock to Walmart and purchase kiddie pools that we hoped would fit the entire family if we squeezed. Montanans are tough, but when it's hot, we are pretty sure that is where it will end for us.

One such summer day, I decided to have a party. We started the day at the river and headed back to our house for dinner. I'd closed all the windows and was crossing my fingers that it had "stayed cool," but when I opened the door it felt like stepping from a temperature-controlled airplane to Houston in August. Our guests sort of collapsed onto couches and stared numbly at the wall nearest them while they sipped lukewarm, iceless water and sweat dripped off their chins. I frantically turned on the fans and threw open the windows, claiming that I felt a "cool breeze."

Aubs helped me set food out and said, "Whoa, it's hot."

Still clinging to the cool breeze narrative and in complete and utter denial, I exclaimed, "Hot? I don't think it's hot; my house stays really nice and cool, actually. It feels pretty nice to me." Sweat burned my eyes as it ran down my nose, and I blinked as she stared at me blankly.

"Okay," she said.

That night when things had finally cooled off, we sat eating ice cream after the other guests had gone home.

"So . . ." she said, giving me the side eye. "You were pretty defensive earlier."

"I was?" I turned quickly.

"My house is so nice and cold!" She raised an eyebrow at me.

"Oh my gosh." I started laughing as I realized the truth in her observation. "You're right, I'm so sorry."

It's been seven years since then, and we still joke about that day. Anytime I'm being what we've coined as "overly positive," she says, "My house is so nice and cool; it's not hot at all," and I realize what I'm doing. I'd had a habit of defensive positivity (also known as total denial) when I was under stress all my life, and I never knew it until she pointed it out.

She could have rolled her eyes and vented to another friend about how I was being weird and defensive. She could have buried her annoyance at me and been perpetually frustrated by that same quirk (because I would have never realized I was doing it unless she said something), but she didn't; she just asked me about it.

If we don't ask the hard questions, and if we don't speak to our friends honestly, how will we grow? If we don't call one another out once in a while, how will we ever see our blind spots, and how will we ever get better at friendship?

I don't know about you, but I value the honest friends I have in my life. It might hurt in the moment, but having people around me who will tell the truth is invaluable. Like Proverbs 27:6 says: "Wounds from a sincere friend are better than many kisses from an enemy" (NLT).

This is important. We have to make sure we get our letters to the right mailbox. If we have a friend who's hurt us (and we value them), we need to talk to them, not to our other friend who has nothing to do with it. Gossip is a false flag of vulnerability. It feels good to vent, but it's not going to get us any closer to either friend. It's not going to get us closer to the friend we have the issue with, and it's not going to get us closer to the friend to whom we're venting.

As Amy always says, we have to RSVP no to drama and stop the gossip with us.

Gossip is fun. There, I said it.

You know what else is probably fun? Going to Bora Bora with the rent money and grocery shopping naked. Probably shouldn't do those things, though.

Gossip is fun, but it's also toxic, and it's not a victimless offense. Remember how I said words are powerful? They are. Gossip isn't just damaging to the people being gossiped about; it's also damaging to you and the person to whom you're talking. Bonding over gossip is like bonding over someone else's story. Those bonds are weak, and they never last long. We have to learn to stop the name-calling and story-spreading when it gets to us.

I've been the gossiper, and I've been the girl who was gossiped about. The first is slimy, and the second is painful. Once you've said words, you can't take them back. You can apologize and say you didn't mean it, but harsh words create wounds that are awfully hard to heal. There's not a single thing I've said with a mean spirit that I don't regret. Gossip only leads to broken hearts and broken friendships.

I say we do it differently.

What if we were defenders of women? What if we were the ones at the table who stood up for the girl who was out of the room? What if we spent our energy being fierce advocates and cheerleaders instead of cynics and critics? What if we weren't threatened by one another? What if we went out of our way to build our sisters up?

It's so easy to be against one another, especially in the age of social media. It's easy to assume the worst about others, to tear others down, to blame, and to find fault (and all from the safety of our own couches and keyboards), but it doesn't have to be that way on our watch.

We get to choose. We get to choose the kind of sisterhood we pass down to the next generation.

We don't have to agree to love everyone.

We don't have to do things the same way.

We don't have to live the same lifestyle to have one another's backs.

The world is watching, and our daughters are watching. Let's use our words to spark one another's flames. Let's resolve conflict bravely, and let's stop gossip when it reaches our doors.

What Now?

Start practicing healthy communication. When we exercise a muscle, it gets stronger.

We can ask questions like:

- "What did you mean when you said that?"
- "Hey, are we good?"
- "Are you upset with me?"
- "When you said that, this is what I heard. Is that what you meant?"
- "What made you react like that?"
- "Have I hurt you?"

We can tell each other how we feel:

- "Hey, when you said/did that, it hurt my feelings."
- "Can we talk about the other day? I felt like things got weird between us."
- "I've been struggling with _____. Can we talk about it?"
- "When you do _____ I feel_____."

We can listen well and apologize sincerely:

- "I was really grumpy today, and I took it out on you; I'm so sorry."
- "Hey, after I said that, I realized it was really insensitive; will you forgive me?"
- "I'm sorry I'm being kinda weird today; I'm not feeling good."
- "You're right. I'm so sorry I did that."
- "Oh my gosh, I can totally see how that came across like that. It wasn't my intention. I'm so sorry."

Communication is a powerful tool. When we ask questions, share how we feel, listen well, and apologize sincerely, it takes our friendships to a whole new level of depth. It can be scary (especially at first), but the reward of connection is precious.

Conclusion

WHEN YOU'RE READY TO DO
THIS FOR REAL

On our first trip together, we met in San Diego.
The weather was balmy, and the taco trucks were plentiful.
We gave our awkward first hug at four o'clock or so in the after-
noon, and by six thirty we were inhaling mountains of french
fries and snort laughing like we'd been doing this for years. By
seven we'd lost our car, and Amy had tried to climb a tree. She
is who she is.

By eight o'clock Amy had learned that Jess cannot both talk
and drive at the same time unless you enjoy going fifteen miles
per hour and passing your hotel forty-seven times. By nine Jess
had learned that there is a big difference between Texas country

music and other country music. By nine thirty Amy had given her earrings away to a complete stranger because the stranger told her they were pretty. By ten, Amy learned that Jess still needed a "bedtime snack" even though she'd already consumed a cheeseburger the size of her head.

After months of calls and texts, meeting in real life felt completely normal and natural—comfortable even. We floated around that town complimenting strangers, laughing at our own jokes (we think we're hilarious), shopping for tacky tourist T-shirts, drinking Diet Cokes, taking awful selfies, and observing that seals, although adorable, smell like nightmares and dirty diapers.

It was the perfect first trip.

The next time we got together was in early March 2020.

Jess was still in complete denial that anything bad was happening, and Amy had packed forty bottles of hand sanitizer and would bust out the Lysol wipes to use on saltshakers and menus every time we ate. She also somehow managed to swing doors open with her elbows and then catch them with her feet, so she never had to touch a doorknob with her hands. Spreading kindness but not germs, y'all. We met in Southern California again, but this time it rained every day like a dreary warning that something ominous was looming.

We holed up in our hotel room for nearly five days watching the world fall apart around us. Every day the news got scarier, and Jess's silver linings started to wane. We still ate tacos (a lot of tacos), we still loved being together, and Amy still built her special pillow fort thingy that she sleeps under. (Yes, this is a thing.)

This time, however, things were obviously a little less

lighthearted. Words didn't flow as easily, the laughs were filled with a more anxious tone. The desserts weren't quite as sweet, and we spent a lot of time on the phone with our families trying to rearrange travel plans and figure out what was going on with our kids' schools.

Our friendship wasn't hard, but the world was hard.

This time Amy learned that Jess needs to go on a run when she's angsty. This time Jess learned that when Amy is scared all she wants to do is snuggle her three babies, hold them close, and shovel chocolate-covered almonds in her face. This time Amy learned that Jess is the exact same way, except she wants to trade the candy for hot CHEETOS. We learned that we both find peace in the sand and in nature. We learned that senseless reality TV is perfect for bingeing when things feel out of control. We learned that we can weather rain and storms and bad news, and that even though these things are awful, they're better with a friend you trust.

And maybe that's what friendship is all about. Maybe that's what it all boils down to. It's about rolling with the good times and standing together through the bad times. It's about the fact that life is messy and hard and wonderful and beautiful and kind of like a roller coaster, and we get to do it all together.

It's about sharing inside jokes and macaroni and cheese for breakfast at a swanky brunch place, and it's also about saying, "Hey, I'm really struggling; I'm just so scared," and holding space for each other through the roaring thunder.

That's the kind of friendships we're after. Even though we're long distance, that's the kind of friendship we've created with each other, and that's what we want for each and every one of you.

Maybe it will build slowly like a steady rain. Maybe it will build quickly like a whirlwind. But have patience, persist, and put in the work because, sister, it is so worth it.

Sunshine makes flowers grow, but full blooms don't happen without a little rain in the mix as well.

The good times are great, but the bad times invite a depth and a closeness into your friendships that you could never find anywhere else. Those friendships—the kind that can endure no matter what the weather is outside—are priceless.

And the best news is that you possess every tool you need to build those friendships right now. God has put everything inside of you that you need, and the fact that you picked this book up in the first place—well, that says a lot. It says:

1. You want good friendships (that's the first thing it takes to make them).
2. You're willing to give and to sacrifice to make those friendships work (that's the second thing it takes).
3. You're willing to learn (that's the last thing it takes).

Being a good friend isn't something you're born with; it's something you develop.

Life is like a road trip. It's not so much about where you're headed as it is about the people you're headed there with. What if the thing that really matters is who we're riding with, who is sitting next to us, who is road-tripping beside us?

We're all so stressed about the destination. We're all so worried about what kind of car we're riding in. Does it look good? Is it big enough? Is it Instagram worthy? Is it fancy enough to make other people jealous? *Haha, take* that *everyone from high school! My car kicks serious booty.*

But what if we've missed the point?

From the time we can talk, we're asked what we want to be when we grow up. In high school there was constant pressure to know: What college do you want to go to? What is your major going to be? If you're not going to college, what kind of trade are you going to learn? Where do you want to live? What kind of job do you want? What kind of life do you want? Never once did anyone ask what kind of people we wanted to do life with.

It turns out, that's one of the most essential pieces.

The message that it all revolves around me and my vision and my future and my career is fine, but it also lends itself to a lonely road. We're made to serve something bigger than just ourselves, and sometimes something "bigger" means serving God and serving the people he has so delicately and thoughtfully placed in our lives.

None of it is by accident.

None of *them* are by accident.

We crave a closeness with other people from the moment we are born. It's in our DNA. When God said it wasn't good for man to be alone, he meant it wasn't good for man to be alone. He never promised it would be easy to find companions or that our attempts at relationship would always work out. He never promised that doing life with others would always be sunshine and hand-holding. He never said people wouldn't break our hearts. But even in all our messes and mistakes, there's still something inside of us created to help one another, carry one another, and connect with one another. So if you're looking for somewhere to start, look for someone to serve.

Whether our purpose is teaching others, building businesses that provide for others, greeting others, encouraging others, hosting others, leading others, writing for others, or raising others—our purpose usually finds a place to land in someone else's hand.

God created us, and he loved us enough to give us other people.

We don't know what stage you're in currently. Maybe you're in a stage full of friends who are tried, true, and real. Maybe you're in a stage with a few newer friends, and you're hopeful these few friends will soon become your people. Or maybe you're in a stage where you're all alone.

Maybe you've lost a friend—something broke in your last friendship and now you feel a little broken too. Maybe insecurity has been getting the best of you or you've been held hostage by your own need to please people. Maybe you keep having the same thing happen over and over, and you know there must be another way.

Maybe you don't know how to move on from the past. Maybe you don't know how to give others grace or you don't know how to give yourself grace. Maybe you're hesitant to dive into a new relationship because the old ones left you feeling like crud— unsure, disappointed, and confused.

No matter where you are right now, no matter what your friend history looks like, no matter how many numbers are in your contact list, there is hope, and you aren't alone.

You can do this.

You can cultivate meaningful relationships. You can find friends who go the distance. You can do life with others, and you can do it well.

It won't be perfect. It won't always work out the way you want. Every once in a while it will probably feel like that one time you forgot to put the lid on your blender and it shot smoothie and ice chunks and pieces of strawberry all over your kitchen cabinets.

But remember there are a million women behind you on the journey, there are a million women ahead, and there are a million women walking beside you at this very moment.

You can do this.

⋘⋘

We started out this book with a prayer for you, and we're going to end on a similar note. Here are a few things that we pray for you. We pray you find

- your place—a space with the ones who feel like home;
- your people—the ones who are for you and with you and in it for the long haul;
- the ones who get you and want you—who keep you around and keep you warm when the world turns cold;
- the ones who let you speak your truth, who know how to disagree in love and how to walk away from an argument but stay close, even when words feel more like stones than bridges;
- the ones who care enough to tell you the truth you need to hear, whether you want to hear it or not;
- the ones who value genuine connection, give more than they take, and take conversations out of the shallow end;

- the ones who make life more fun;
- the ones who give you grace when you need to come undone;
- the ones who save you a seat and offer you an invitation and miss you when you can't be there;
- the ones who point you to the right path when you've gone off-roading and defend you when you aren't around;
- the ones who stay and are loyal;
- the ones who love you—who truly, truly love you—and show you in a way that reminds you there's a God in heaven who loves you even more; and
- the ones who point you to him, whose light helps you shine brighter, and who remind you exactly who you are, even when you might have forgotten.

We pray they see you. We pray they know you. We pray their connection transforms you in the best way possible. Most of all, we pray that when you find them, you'll have the courage to give everything they've given to you back tenfold.

What Now?

Connecting with other people was always meant to be an adventure. What a wild ride to get to see God's glorious creativity in the faces of everyone around you. What a privilege to sit with them, talk with them, and hear their stories. What a joy just to connect with them. Our connections with them were meant to be teeny-tiny reflections of God's connection with us. He lets us love them and serve them and hang out with them. Connection is not something to be dreaded or taken lightly. It is sacred, and it is special.

Get out there and have fun. Meet people. Take chances. Ask questions. Bring them coffee. Invite them into your home. Invite them into your life. Look them in the eyes. Say yes to having dinner together and leave the laundry for later. Have good conversations. Listen well. Laugh a lot, and learn everything you can. Order the queso. Be brave, and let them see the real you. We don't have to have friends. We *get* to have friends. And yeah, it's tricky, and it's weird sometimes, but what a blessing. Enjoy people. We think they'll enjoy you right back, and that's how a sisterhood is built: with intention, with honesty, with vulnerability, and with joy.

Notes

Chapter 2: When You're Alone and It All Kinda Sucks

1. Mattie Quinn, "Loneliness May Be a Bigger Public Health Threat Than Smoking or Obesity," Governing: The Future of States and Localities, April 20, 2018, https://www.governing.com/archive/gov-the -loneliness-epidemic.html.

2. Vivek Murthy, "Work and the Loneliness Epidemic," *Harvard Business Review*, September 26, 2017, https://hbr.org/2017/09/work-and-the -loneliness-epidemic.

3. Miller McPherson, Lynn Smith-Lovin, and Matthew E. Brashears, "Social Isolation in America: Changes in Core Discussion Networks over Two Decades," *American Sociological Review* 71, no. 3 (June 2006): 353–75, https://doi.org/10.1177/000312240607100301.

4. *Cigna 2018 U.S. Loneliness Index*, https://www.cigna.com/assets/docs /newsroom/loneliness-survey-2018-updated-fact-sheet.pdf.

Chapter 3: When You Can't Amazon Prime Your Friendships

1. Jeffrey A. Hall, "How Many Hours Does It Take to Make a Friend?," *Journal of Social and Personal Relationships* 36, no. 4 (April 2019): 1278–96, https://doi.org/10.1177/0265407518761225.

Chapter 4: When Insecurity Reigns Supreme

1. *Mean Girls*, directed by Mark Waters, written by Tina Fey, starring Rachel McAdams and Lindsay Lohan (Los Angeles, CA: Paramount Pictures, 2004), Blu-ray Disc, 19:44.

Chapter 5: When You're Pretty Sure You've Been Duped

1. "Lonely," featuring Benny Blanco, Spotify, track 16 on Justin Bieber, *Justice*, Def Jam Recordings, 2021.
2. Cigna, "Cigna Takes Action to Combat the Rise of Loneliness and Improve Mental Wellness in America," news release, January 23, 2020, https://www.cignabigpicture.com/issues/march-2020/cigna-takes -action-to-combat-the-rise-of-loneliness-and-improve-mental -wellness-in-america1/.

Chapter 8: When You're Stuck on the Outside

1. Christine Ro, "Dunbar's Number: Why We Can Only Maintain 150 Relationships," BBC Future, October 9, 2019, https://www.bbc.com /future/article/20191001-dunbars-number-why-we-can-only -maintain-150-relationships.

Chapter 13: When Your Mouth Gets Sticky and Words Get Hard

1. "Bully a Plant: Say No to Bullying," video shared by IKEA UAE, April 30, 2018, on YouTube, https://www.youtube.com/watch?v =Yx6UgfQreYY.

About the Authors

Amy Weatherly is a Texas girl through and through, which is where she lives with her husband, three kids, and two rescue dogs—Lou and Brewster. She is passionate about helping women embrace courage, confidence, and purpose for their life, and she does it with a quick wit and down-to-earth sense of humor. She has written for the *Today Show*, MSN.com, *Good Morning America*, Yahoo.com, and Love What Matters.

Jess Johnston lives in Southern California with her husband and four kids who are the loves of her life. Her favorite thing to do is sit around a table with her best friends, eating nachos and laughing until her stomach hurts. She has been a top contributor to publications such as *HuffPo*, *Scary Mommy*, and *Motherly*, and has been honored with *Motherly*'s Writer of the Year Award.

Go Deeper with the Companion Workbook

The perfect "sister" to *I'll Be There (But I'll Be Wearing Sweatpants)*, this workbook is your personal account of getting to the place you most want to be—standing beside women who encourage you, lift you, see you, and remind you that you aren't alone in this crazy, messy, rollercoaster life. Addressing the incredible value of friendship, this workbook provides space and structure and focus for the practical steps on how to get there. Inside these pages, you will discover the thirteen most common obstacles to connection and apply actionable steps to solve each one.

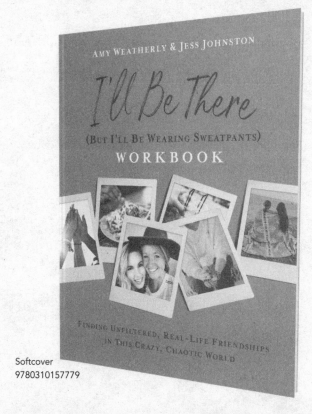

Softcover
9780310157779

Available now at your favorite bookstore.

HarperChristian Resources